THE
QUICK
&EASY
COOKBOOK

JOAN SAVIN

KEEP COOL

If you are tired of mixing, beating, clarifying, reducing liquids, and simmering for hours on end . . .

If you find no satisfaction in mounding up loads of dirty dishes and pots for each dish prepared . . .

If you'd rather entertain your guests than stand in the kitchen cooking while you *listen* to your party . . .

If you find you simply don't have the time to cook the kind of food you'd really like to make . . .

If you dislike standing over a hot stove when you could be enjoying a cool drink . . .

Don't give up good cooking. Simply give up outdated, old-fashioned cooking methods. Substitute the modern, quick and easy way of cooking that makes the most efficient use of today's convenience foods.

Contents

Foreword

The first glimmering of this book occurred the day I leafed through a ragged clipping collection of my currently favored recipes and discovered they were all of a kind—quick and easy. These recipes, quite unlike the ones I had used exclusively just a few years before, were the no-work variety that contained at least one prepared food ingredient.

The prepared (or convenience) foods crowding more and more supermarket shelves come canned, freeze-dried, frozen, dehydrated and refrigerated. These are the foods of the future, and a great many of them have already arrived. They are pre-cleaned, pre-squeezed, pre-boned, pre-grated, pre-cut, pre-measured, pre-mixed, pre-cooked, etc. or combinations thereof, and minimum preparation is all that's required of the cook.

In this comprehensive collection of timesaving recipes you'll find original recipes, old favorites that are classics of their kind, and the newest recipes developed by the manufacturers of prepared foods. There are "secret" recipes, successful recipes lent by generous friends, non-exotic recipes for everyday cooking, and fancy party recipes.

The two major criteria for recipe excellence were substantial and non-illusory reduction of work time, and a high degree of homemade flavor. The cooking time (i.e. baking, simmering, chilling, etc., time that doesn't actively involve the cook) varies from instant to hours, but always the cook is spared most of the time-consuming work element of cooking.

The chapter on How To Spend Less Time In The Kitchen is a series of time-saving techniques written especially for the busy people who spend most of their day outside the kitchen and those who would like to find their way out.

Definition of Terms

Note: All food products used in the recipes in this book are available in local supermarkets. If your favorite store does not stock a particular item ask the manager to order it for you or try another chain.

t = teaspoon
T = tablespoon
C = cup

Servings: The servings recommendations in this book are adult sized and generous. Meat servings (boneless) are approximately a half pound per person; vegetables, side dishes and salads, generally three quarters cup per person. Serving proportions are always arbitrary because we are faced with an unanswerable question: Who are the eaters? Are they male or female? Big? Small? Growing? Dieting? Young? Old? Active? It all makes a difference when you're planning meals and therein lies the dilemma.

Prepare as directed: When a packaged ingredient is followed with these words, refer to, and follow, the directions on the box, can or envelope. When the words *do not appear* expect either to use the product as is, i.e. straight out of the package, or prepared somewhat differently from the package directions.

Canned fruits and *vegetables* are used drained unless recipe says "plus juice". The one exception is canned tomatoes, which should be used with liquid.

Canned soups are condensed unless otherwise indicated. They are used in their condensed state in the recipe unless directed to the contrary.

Oven baked dishes, casseroles, etc. are cooked *uncovered* unless directions state otherwise.

Package and can weights are approximate. A slight weight variance in commercial products should not significantly change the finished dish.

Sour cream is dairy sour cream, a commercial product, not the home variety.

MSG monosodium glutamate: a well known brand is Accent.

Large eggs are used throughout.

Bread crumbs are the finely-ground packaged variety unless otherwise indicated.

Brown sugar is measured packed in all recipes.

Where *evaporated milk* is called for, products such as Milnot may be substituted.

Rice-macaroni mix refers to products such as Rice-a-roni.

Whipped dessert mix refers to products such as Whip and Chill, etc.

Whipped topping mix is a whipped cream substitute such as Dream Whip. One envelope, prepared, makes two cups of topping.

Non-dairy whipped topping is a frozen ready-to-eat whipped cream substitute, such as Cool Whip. It may be refrigerated for a period of two weeks.

Seasoned coating mix refers to products such as Shake'n Bake.

Golden egg custard mix is a Jello mix. It is cooked in a saucepan much like pudding and pie filling mixes.

Real egg custard mix is essentially an egg substitute and is *baked* rather than cooked on the stove.

Chocolate drink mix is a product like Nestles' Quik or Hershey's Instant Cocoa.

Liquid baking chocolate (unsweetened chocolate flavor) is Choco-bake, Redi-Blend, etc.

Instant rice is a pre-cooked rice such as Minute Rice.

Instant minced onions are dehydrated onion flakes.

Imitation bacon bits are also called Bac-os, etc.

Lemon-lime carbonated beverage is 7/Up or a similar product.

Mexicorn is a canned combination of whole kernel corn, diced pimento and green pepper.

Chapter 1

How to Spend Less Time in the Kitchen

OUT OF TIME SAVERS—OUT OF LUCK

One of the wilder frustrations for the person who needs to cook fast is running out of prepared foods. Unless you remember to keep shelves well stocked with canned, frozen, freeze-dried, dehydrated and refrigerator foods, you will find yourself cooking the old-fashioned, time-consuming way. The solution? Take time to save time. Spend a few extra minutes each week making sure your shopping list is really complete. A carefully itemized shopping list of time-saver foods can save actual hours of cooking time. It may also save a second shopping trip.

ASK THE BUTCHER TO DO IT

Attractive, idea-sparking and quickly chosen prepackaged meats are the modern wonder of the supermarket world. But standardized cuts of meat locked in plastic prisons can be intimidating. Do you find only 2 lb. packages of ground beef when your recipe calls for 1½ lbs.? Do you encounter only large pieces of sirloin when you need your steak sliced for Stroganoff? Prefer your chicken breasts boned? Ring the bell! Call the butcher! He's back there someplace just waiting to give you time-saving, personalized service. Ask him to prepare, weigh, and wrap your meat purchases according to *your* specifications. Boned chicken breasts may require an extra friendly butcher on a not so busy day, so shop for these or place an order early in the week. Now, while the butcher is busy preparing your order don't just stand there! Use the waiting time to shop the other aisles.

LETTER CLIPS FOR ENVELOPE FOODS

The proliferation of modern foods packaged in envelopes demands a redesigning of kitchen cabinets, it seems to me, for envelopes are not made to be stored on shelves. They won't stand up, they don't stack, and they're easily lost. One way to solve the problem is to clip envelopes together with letter clips and hang them from cup hooks which have been screwed to the inside of cabinet doors. Another solution is a 4 x 6-inch card file box which will hold as many as a dozen envelopes of varied sizes.

WASH BEFORE STORING
Someday the purchase of thoroughly washed, ready-to-eat fresh fruits and vegetables will be taken for granted. But until that Great Day arrives the washing task is a do-it-yourself project for the busy homemaker. Save time by washing and drying fresh produce (except asparagus, broccoli and berries) immediately after shopping and before storing in the refrigerator. Refrigerator drawers stay cleaner longer and you eliminate innumerable trips from the refrigerator to the sink for individual wash jobs.

FILE FASTER
Here's a quick and easy way to file recipe clippings. *Do not recopy;* instead paste, glue, tape or staple the recipe to a file card (preferably the 4 x 6-inch size). Or use the adhesive backed transparent plastic found in hardware and department stores. Peel the backing off, slap on a recipe face down, and cut around the edge. You've created your own file card—one that's impervious to use, time and grease spots. Use the same method for smaller clippings: Leave a ½-inch or wider border of peeled plastic and affix to a file card.

EXERCISE YOUR MEASURING EYE
Ever notice that the fastest cooks seldom use measuring devices? This talent is a result of experience, familiarity with a recipe, plus a great degree of cooking confidence. And it can happen to you. After using a recipe once or twice (so you know how it's supposed to taste) begin training by eye-measuring the ingredients one would ordinarily measure with measuring spoons. Use the bottle cap as a measuring device for liquids contained in bottles (extracts, etc.), or pour directly from the bottle into a mixing spoon. Shake dashes of dry ingredients such as spices into a mix-

ing spoon. *Notice that the eye-measured ingredients are not poured directly into the mixing bowl.* Using the mixing spoon as an intermediate container for the eye-measured ingredients provides a safety control since an over-measure can be dumped in the sink and no harm done.

What is the measure of a bottle cap? A dash? If your eye can't gauge it pre-measure your dashes and the volume of various bottlecaps and find out. You have only a time-consuming habit to lose!

MIX IT IN A MOLD

Not extra fancy, but a nice little timesaver. When preparing a simple molded salad combine the ingredients in a small circumference, deep bowl that will do double duty as a salad mold. Chill, invert on a serving plate, instant mold!

COOK IT IN A CASSEROLE

Like instant molds, casseroles operate as time-motion savers through the multiple function of a single container. In the most efficient use of a casserole the food is *combined* as well as cooked and served in the same vessel. When a casserole recipe calls for the prior cooking of one ingredient a flameproof casserole will permit this performance on a stove burner and eliminate the need of a separate saucepan. (The fancy saucepan or frying pan that doubles as a serving dish is another timesaver in the same category.)

The advantages of cooking in a casserole are not limited to foods cooked in sauces. Next time you prepare an oven meal try the casserole method with frozen vegetables. Place them in a covered casserole, add a tablespoon or two of butter, season, and place in the oven to cook with the rest of the meal. Thirty minutes at 375° F. or 45 minutes at 350° F. will do it nicely.

FORGET IT IN THE OVEN

One of the great benefits of oven cooking is being able to forget about the meal while the oven does the work. No watchful stirring the pot, no grease spatter burns while standing sentinel over the grill, nor careful checking liquid reduction every ten minutes or so. While the food is in the oven the time is your own—to accomplish other things or just to sit and relax a bit.

15

Although oven cooking is usually associated with casseroles and roasts, many foods that are ordinarily pan fried adapt beautifully to the oven-fry method. Hamburgers, meatballs, chicken, bacon, and French toast are a few examples. The technique is especially practical when there are large amounts to be cooked.

FREEZE MEAL-SIZE PORTIONS

Foil wrapped and frozen in meal-size portions, rolls and pre-sliced bread travel effortlessly from the freezer to the oven to the table. Celery, green pepper, and onion can be diced and frozen in pre-measured amounts in plastic sacks, ready for last minute additions to stews, chop sueys, and casserole dishes (Not recommended for salads).

Preparing a casserole? Mix a double batch; bake one and freeze the other. Here's another way to create your own convenience foods—the pre-cooked variety. When storing leftover turkey and other roasted meats slice the meat or cut in cubes. In separate packets freeze the amounts called for in your favorite recipes. Do the same with leftover vegetables and stuffing. Gravy, too, should be freeze-stored in meal-sized portions, or frozen in the proper proportion with leftover meats.

Single-serving sized leftovers may be frozen as they accumulate in resurrected frozen dinner trays. When all the courses are filled, you've got yourself a homemade TV dinner.

TOSS IT AWAY

High on the list of successful timesavers is the whole family of paper, plastic and foil disposables. Throwaway cake and pie pans, foil muffin cups, broiler pans, roasting pans and pizza pans eliminate a time-consuming dishwashing job.

No longer relegated to summertime picnics and children's parties, the table setting disposables are available in supermarkets all year round. The hurried homemaker uses them at every opportunity. Dinner, luncheon and breakfast can be served on 9-inch plates, salads and desserts on the 6-inch size. Paper and plastic cups, functionally designed to hold hot or cold beverages, provide efficient containers for soups, too. For breakfast cereal, sliced fruits, puddings, etc. there are plasticized paper bowls.

Tables can be attractively laid with the pretty new paper placemats, tablecloths and napkins now available in a wide choice of sizes, textures, colors and printed designs. A paper-clad table practically guarantees one less washing machine load a week and eliminates the ironing that follows inevitably.

Chapter 2

Meats and Main Dishes

Beef
Chicken and Other Birds
Pork, Ham and Sauces to Serve with Baked Ham
Veal, Lamb and Chop Suey
Fish and Shellfish
Spaghetti Sauces and Lasagna
Chili and South of the Border Dishes

What to serve for dinner? That is the inescapable question we cooks face daily (weekly, if we're really efficient)! Use this chapter as your menu decision starting point. Once the main course choice is made you'll find the battle is half won. Ideas for the other courses will slip neatly into view, and that nagging question is answered—at least until tomorrow.

BEEF

In our hurry it is easy to overlook the wealth of excellent recipes that may be found on convenience food packages. Therefore, the best of these recipes have been included in this book. Foil-Baked Pot Roast, beautifully brown, tender and onion flavored through and through, is one of these.

Bits Of Beef In Wine Sauce

2 lbs. beef stew, cut in 1-inch cubes
1 can (8 oz.) tomato sauce
1½ C water
½ C sherry
1 envelope onion soup mix

Combine all ingredients in a 2-qt. covered casserole. Bake 2 hours at 325° F. Expect a liquid reduction in the sauce. Serves 4 to 6.

18

Easy Sauerbraten

Use Bits Of Beef In Wine Sauce recipe, but substitute ½ C wine vinegar for the sherry, and add ½ t garlic salt.

Beef Stew

2 lbs. beef stew, cut in 1½-in cubes
3 T flour
3 T oil
1 envelope beef stew seasoning mix
3 C water
1 bay leaf
1 bag (1½ lbs.) frozen stew vegetables
1½ t salt

Sprinkle stew meat with flour. Heat oil in a 3-qt. Dutch oven and brown the meat. Add the beef stew seasoning mix, water and bay leaf, cover and simmer 1½ hours. Add frozen stew vegetables and salt, bring to a boil and simmer 45 minutes more. Serves 4 to 6.

Laura's Beef Stew Gourmet

3 lbs. beef stew, cut in 1-inch cubes
1 can (10½ oz.) onion soup (liquid)
1 can (10½ oz.) cream of mushroom soup
1 can (4 oz.) sliced mushrooms
1 C port wine
1 t salt
¼ t pepper

Combine all ingredients in a covered casserole. Bake 2 hours at 325° F. If desired, cook the stew the night before, cutting cooking time to 1½ hours. Refrigerate. The following evening, pop the casserole into the oven for 45 minutes. Serves 6 to 8.

19

Beef Stew and Biscuits

2 cans (1½ lbs. each) beef stew
1 pkg. (9 oz.) frozen onions in cream sauce, prepared as
    directed
1 pkg. (10 oz.) frozen peas
1 t basil
1 pkg. refrigerator biscuits, flaky style

In a flameproof casserole, combine beef stew, onions, peas
and ½ t basil. Bring to a boil and simmer 5 minutes. Top
with biscuits, sprinkle remaining basil over all. Bake as directed on biscuit package. Note: It is important that stew
mixture be very hot before topping with the biscuits. The
heat is required to cook the bottom of the biscuits properly. Serves 4.

Old Fashioned Beef Stew

2 cans (19 oz. each) beef stew
1 C chopped apple
¼ C raisins
¼ t cinnamon

Combine all ingredients and heat slowly to bubbling.
Serves 4.

Liver Julienne

1 lb. calves' liver, sliced in thin strips
2 T butter
1 envelope onion gravy mix
¾ C water
½ C sour cream

Brown liver in butter (about 5 minutes.) Add gravy mix
and water. Bring to a boil, stirring constantly. Simmer 5
minutes. Just before serving stir in sour cream. Heat but
do not boil. Serves 2 to 3.

Ellie's Chinese Stew (Round Steak Orientale)

2 lbs. round steak
2 T flour
Salt and pepper to taste
2 T oil
1 can (10½ oz.) onion soup (liquid)
1 soup can water
2 T soy sauce
¼ C dehydrated green pepper
1 can (6 oz.) water chestnuts, sliced

Cut steak in strips ¾ inch wide and coat with flour. Salt and pepper lightly. Brown in oil. Add soup, water and soy sauce. Cover and simmer for about 1 hour, or until tender, adding water as necessary. Add green pepper and water chestnuts during last 5 minutes of cooking. Serves 4 to 6.

Beef Stroganoff

2 lbs. sirloin steak, cut in half-inch strips
3 T each, flour and oil
2/3 C frozen chopped onion
1 can (4½ oz.) sliced mushrooms, or ½ lb. fresh sliced
1 t salt
1 t Worcestershire sauce
2 C sour cream

Coat meat with flour. In a large skillet heat oil; add meat, onion and mushrooms. Sauté quickly over high heat just until brown. Remove skillet from heat. Stir in sour cream, salt and Worcestershire sauce. Heat through but do not boil. Transfer to a warm serving dish or a chafing dish. Prepare 2 C of instant rice in the same skillet (don't wash it out) following package directions. Spoon rice around meat mixture to serve. Serves 4 to 6.

Two imperatives should guarantee the success of your Beef Stroganoff. 1. Cook the steak only as long as it takes to brown on high heat. The meat will be medium rare and tender. 2. Always heat a sour cream mixture to *just below* boiling. It will separate (curdle) if allowed to boil.

Meat Loaf #1

1½ C herb-seasoned stuffing mix
½ C warm water
1 envelope onion soup mix
1 can (8 oz.) tomato sauce
1 egg
1½ lbs. ground beef

Moisten stuffing mix with water. Stir in remaining ingredients and turn into a shallow baking pan. Form into a loaf and bake 50 to 60 minutes at 350° F. Serves 4.

Meat Loaf #2

1 to 2 lbs. ground beef
1 small can (6 oz.) evaporated milk
1 envelope onion soup mix

Combine ingredients, shape into a loaf, and bake 45 minutes at 350° F. Serves 2 to 4. (Figure a half pound of meat per person.)

Beef Bourgogne

2 to 2½ lbs. frozen beef and gravy*
1 jar (4 oz.) sliced mushrooms
2 T butter
¼ C burgundy or claret

Heat beef and gravy according to package directions, but cook 10 minutes less than recommended time. Sauté drained mushrooms in butter 3 minutes, but reserve liquid. Add mushrooms, butter, mushroom liquid and wine to beef and gravy. (If necessary, transfer beef and gravy mixture to a saucepan or flameproof serving dish.) Heat through and serve. Serves 4 to 6.

* Any sliced beef and gravy product may be used in this recipe as long as the weight is within ½ lb, more or less. Three C of leftover beef (sliced) and 2 cans of beef gravy also may be used.

Liver and Onions

1 lb. calves' liver
2 T butter
1 can (10½ oz.) onion gravy
2 T chili sauce

Brown liver in butter. Add gravy and chili sauce. Cover and simmer 15 minutes or until tender. Serves 2 to 3.

Meatballs and Baked Beans

1 can (21 oz.) baked beans, drained
1 can (1 lb.) meatballs and gravy
1 T instant minced onions
1 T Worcestershire sauce
½ C barbecue sauce

Combine all ingredients in a baking dish or bean pot. Bake uncovered 30 to 40 minutes at 350° F. Serves 2 to 3.

Sara's Welcome Neighbor! Casserole

1 lb. ground beef
½ C frozen chopped onion
1 can (10½ oz.) tomato soup
1 C large curd cottage cheese
Dash garlic powder
1 t Italian seasoning
¼ C grated Parmesan cheese
1 pkg. refrigerator biscuits

Brown beef and onion in a flameproof casserole. Add soup, cottage cheese, garlic and Italian seasoning. Heat to boiling. Sprinkle Parmesan cheese over top. Cut 5 or 6 biscuits in half and arrange around edge of casserole. Bake 20 minutes at 375° F. Bake remaining biscuits on a piece of foil at the same time. Send them along with the casserole to your new neighbor on move-in day. Serves 3.

Sliced Beef Provencale

2 to 2½ lbs. frozen sliced beef and gravy*
1 can (8 oz.) tomato sauce
1 t salt
½ t thyme
1 bay leaf
1 garlic clove, crushed
¼ t freshly ground pepper

Heat beef and gravy according to package directions. Ten minutes before completely heated through, remove from container (or heating pouches) and turn into a chafing dish. Stir in remaining ingredients. Simmer 15 minutes. Serves 4 to 5.

Homemade Hash

Here's a home-style hash without the bother of grinding the meat.

1 can (12 oz.) corned beef, flaked
2 C mashed potatoes (4 servings instant mashed potatoes, prepared as directed)
2 T chopped green onion or frozen chopped chives
1 t parsley flakes
1 egg, slightly beaten
Salt and pepper to taste
Butter

Combine all ingredients except butter. Shape into patties and sauté in butter. Brown both sides and serve. Serves 3.

Hash Stroganoff

1 can (15½ oz.) roast beef or corned beef hash (chilled)
2 t butter
1 can (2 oz.) sliced mushrooms
1 C sour cream (or sour half and half)
Paprika to taste

Cut chilled hash in 4 to 6 slices and arrange in shallow casserole. Heat in a 350° F. oven for 15 minutes. Meanwhile brown mushrooms in butter. Remove from heat and add sour cream. Pour this mixture around hash slices and continue baking another 10 minutes. Sprinkle with paprika before serving. Serves 2.

Foil-Baked Pot Roast

3 or 4 lb. chuck roast (or any less tender cut)
1 envelope onion soup mix

Place roast on a large piece of heavy duty foil, sprinkle with dry onion soup mix. Wrap, sealing with double folds. (If regular weight foil is used instead, place wrapped roast in a shallow pan to collect possible leaking juices.) Bake 2 hours at 350° F. For variety, add a jar (any size) of sliced mushrooms or a can of cream of mushroom soup with the onion soup mix. Serves 6 to 8.

Beef Rolls

1 to 1½ lbs. minute steaks
1 C stuffing mix, prepared as directed
1 can (10 oz.) beef gravy
1 envelope onion soup mix
1 C water
¼ t nutmeg

In center of each steak place a spoonful of prepared stuffing. Roll up each steak and secure with a toothpick. Place in an ovenproof dish. Combine remaining ingredients and bring to a boil, stirring constantly. Pour sauce over meat rolls, cover and bake 30 minutes at 375° F. Baste once after 15 minutes. Serves 2 to 4.

* * * * *

CHICKEN AND OTHER BIRDS

Once upon a time, back in the "old days," chicken dinner was a Sunday Special, and children sitting at the Sunday dinner table pondered the possibilities of developing a three-legged chicken. Today when chicken is served, all the kids get a drumstick, Mama's rescued the budget, and it's likely to be any day of the week.

Chicken Cacciatore

1 frying chicken, cut up
½ C frozen chopped onion
2 T oil
1 envelope spaghetti sauce mix
1 can (6 oz.) tomato paste
1½ C water
1 can (4 oz.) mushrooms

Brown chicken and onion in oil in a large skillet. Push to one side and add remaining ingredients, except for mushrooms. Stir to mix. Cover and simmer 45 minutes. Add mushrooms during last 5 minutes of cooking. Serves 3 to 4.

Oven Chicken Supreme

½ C instant potato flakes
½ C grated Parmesan cheese
¼ C melted butter
1 frying chicken, cut up
Salt to taste

Combine potato flakes and cheese on a sheet of waxed paper. Melt butter in a large shallow baking pan. (A jelly roll pan is perfect.) Roll each piece of chicken in butter and coat with potato and cheese mixture. Place coated chicken in the baking pan, sprinkle lightly with salt, and bake 1 hour at 350° F. Serves 3 to 4.

Arroz Con Pollo

4 T butter
1 frying chicken, cut up and seasoned
1 pkg. (8 oz.) chicken-flavored rice-macaroni mix
2 C water
1 can (1 lb.) tomatoes
½ t salt

Melt butter in a 3-qt. flameproof casserole; brown chicken. Remove the chicken from the pan. Brown the rice-macaroni. Stir in the contents of flavor packet, water, tomatoes and salt. Arrange chicken pieces in this mixture, cover, and bake 40 minutes at 350° F. Remove cover during the last ten minutes. Serves 3 or 4.

Party Breast of Chicken

A most successful dinner party entree! Remember to have your friendly butcher bone the breasts.

¼ C dried imported mushrooms
½ C water
8 whole chicken breasts, boned
¼ C butter
2 cans (10½ oz. each) cream of chicken soup
1 jar (4 oz.) sliced mushrooms
¼ C sherry
½ C to ¾ C bottled hollandaise sauce (or your own recipe)

Soak the dried mushrooms in the ½ C of water for one hour. Brown breasts in butter. Add chicken soup, dried mushrooms and the water in which they were soaked. Simmer, covered, for 20 minutes, adding water as necessary. Stir in the sliced mushrooms and sherry and simmer another five minutes. Arrange the chicken breasts with sauce on a large serving platter. Spread breasts with hollandaise sauce and place under the broiler for just a minute or two until bubbly and brown. Serve with instant rice. Serves 8 to 10.

Chicken en Casserole

1 frying chicken, cut up
1 can (10½ oz.) cream of chicken soup
1 can (10½ oz.) onion soup (liquid)
½ C sherry
1 t parsley flakes
½ t salt
¼ t pepper
Paprika to taste

Combine all ingredients but paprika in a 2- to 3-qt. heavy casserole. Cover and bake 1½ hours at 350° F. Sprinkle with paprika before serving. If desired, the chicken may be browned in a small amount of butter or oil before adding the other ingredients. Reduce baking time to 1 hour. Serves 3 or 4.

Oven Fried Chicken

Much of the fun of time-saver cooking is discovering that the easiest recipes, like the following for Oven Fried Chicken Supreme, are often the very best of all.

Basic Oven Fried Chicken

Frying chicken, cut up
Salt, pepper, and seasoned salt
Do not flour

Sprinkle chicken with seasonings. Place chicken pieces skin side up on a cookie sheet. Bake 1 hour at 350° F. There is no need for butter or oil; the chicken skin contains its own fat. It is not necessary to turn the pieces during the baking process. (This rule applies to all oven-fried chicken recipes.) After an hour in the oven, the chicken will be crisp and brown. The children love it, and it couldn't be easier, less caloric or more digestible.

28

Ila's Chicken Divine

2 pkgs. (10 oz. each) frozen broccoli spears
4 to 6 whole chicken breasts, boned and skinned
2 cans (10½ oz. each) cream of chicken soup
1 C mayonnaise
1 T lemon juice
1 C grated Cheddar cheese
½ C bread crumbs
1 t curry powder

Cook broccoli as directed, but reduce cooking time to 2 minutes. Transfer broccoli to a greased 2½-qt. casserole or an 8 x 12-inch baking pan. Steam cook chicken breasts 20 minutes. Arrange breasts over broccoli. Combine soup, mayonnaise and lemon juice and pour this mixture over chicken. Sprinkle grated cheese on top, followed by a mixture of crumbs and curry powder. Bake 30 minutes at 350° F. Serves 4 to 6.

Oven-Fried Chicken Italienne

1 can (10½ oz.) cream of mushroom soup
¼ C milk
2 cut-up frying chickens
1 C Italian-seasoned bread crumbs

Dilute mushroom soup with milk. Coat chicken pieces with this mixture and then roll in seasoned bread crumbs. Bake in a shallow pan for 1 hour at 350° F. Serves 6 to 8.

Baked Chicken Livers

¾ lb. chicken livers
¼ C soy sauce
1 pkg. (2⅜ oz.) seasoned coating mix for chicken

Moisten livers with soy sauce. Shake livers and coating mix in plastic bag as directed. Place on a baking sheet and bake 15 minutes at 400° F. Serves 2.

Baked Chicken in Sour Cream

3 whole chicken breasts (or 1 cup-up fryer)
Seasoned flour
¼ C butter
1 jar (4 oz.) sliced mushrooms
1 can (10½ oz.) cream of mushroom soup
1 C sour cream

Dredge chicken in seasoned flour. Melt butter in shallow baking pan. Roll chicken in melted butter and arrange pieces in single layer, skin side down. Bake for 30 minutes at 350° F. Remove from oven and turn skin side up. Cover with mixture of soup, sour cream and mushrooms (drained). Return to oven and bake another 40 minutes. Serves 3 to 4.

Fried Chicken Breasts Oven Style

1 egg, slightly beaten
2 T milk
1 C potato flakes or granules
1 envelope cheese-garlic salad dressing mix
4 whole chicken breasts
¼ C butter

Combine egg and milk; set aside. Combine potato flakes and dressing mix. Dip breasts in egg mixture and roll in potato mixture. Melt butter in shallow baking pan. Arrange chicken breasts in butter. Bake at 400° F. for 50 minutes. Serves 4 to 6.

Crispy Chicken Drumsticks

1 C corn flake crumbs
½ C grated Parmesan cheese
Salt and pepper to taste
3 to 4 lbs. chicken legs
1 C boiled salad dressing or mayonnaise

Combine crumbs, cheese and a light sprinkling of salt and pepper. Coat chicken with salad dressing and dip each piece in the crumb mixture. Bake in a shallow pan 1 hour at 350° F. Serves 4 to 6.

Easy Chicken Sauté

1 frying chicken, quartered
¼ C butter
Seasoned salt to taste
1 can (4 oz.) shoestring potatoes

Brown chicken in butter in a heavy skillet. Sprinkle with seasoned salt, cover, and cook over low heat until tender, about 30 minutes. Add shoestring potatoes and toss with pan juices to heat (about 5 minutes). Serves 3 to 4.

BONED CHICKEN AND LEFTOVER TURKEY DISHES

Chicken Tetrazzini

½ lb. spaghetti, cooked according to package directions
    and drained
1 envelope Italian-style spaghetti sauce mix
1 C chicken broth
1 C evaporated milk
2 T butter
2 to 3 C diced or sliced cooked chicken or turkey
1 jar (4 oz.) sliced mushrooms, plus liquid
¼ C grated Parmesan cheese

Arrange cooked spaghetti on bottom and around sides of greased 2-qt. casserole. Combine sauce mix, broth, milk and butter. Heat to boiling and stir constantly. Simmer 5 minutes. Add chicken, mushrooms and liquid to sauce. Pour over spaghetti; sprinkle with cheese. Bake 20 minutes in a 400° F. oven. Serves 4 to 6.

Pineapple Chicken Chow Mein

1 can (1 lb.) chicken chow mein
1 can (8 oz.) pineapple tidbits
½ C finely sliced celery
1 T soy sauce

Combine all ingredients in a saucepan. Heat slowly to bubbling and serve over chow mein noodles. If more meat is desired, add 1 C diced, cooked and seasoned chicken. The celery should remain crunchy and green. Serves 2.

Turkey Bake

1 envelope chicken-rice soup mix, prepared as directed
4 eggs
2 C herb-seasoned croutons, or stuffing mix
3 C leftover turkey, diced
½ C celery, diced
1 jar (2 oz.) chopped pimiento
1 t salt
1 t MSG

Allow prepared soup to cool. In a large mixing bowl, beat eggs until foamy. Stir in soup and remaining ingredients. Spread in a well greased 8 x 12-inch baking pan. Bake 50 minutes at 325° F. To serve, cut in squares and top each serving with hot leftover gravy or the following Chicken Giblet Gravy. Serves 6 to 8.

Chicken Giblet Gravy

1 can (10½ oz.) cream of chicken soup
1 can (10½ oz.) giblet gravy

Combine soup and gravy; heat. If a thinner sauce is preferred add 1/3 C milk. Serves 8.

OTHER BIRDS

Turkey Roast and Gravy

1 boneless turkey roast (2 to 6 lbs.)
3 T pan drippings
1 can (10½ oz.) giblet gravy
1 can (10½ oz.) golden mushroom soup (or cream of
    chicken soup)
½ C water
Freshly ground pepper to taste

Roast the boneless turkey roast according to package directions. When done transfer to a hot platter and let stand while making the gravy. Pour off all but 3 T of drippings from the roasting pan. Combine drippings with remaining ingredients; heat to boiling while stirring constantly. Serve the turkey roast and gravy with Stuffing Casserole p. 98. Servings: allow ½ lb. per person.

Rock Cornish Game Hens with Wine Sauce

The wine sauce may be made with the same wine you plan to serve with the dinner.

6 to 8 frozen rock Cornish game hens (16 to 24 oz. each)
Salt
¼ C butter, melted
Wine Sauce:
Giblets
1 t salt
1 can (10½ oz.) cream of chicken soup
1 can (10½ oz.) mushroom gravy
¼ t freshly ground pepper
¼ to ½ C dry sherry

Thaw game hens completely. Remove giblet bag from each hen. Sprinkle with salt inside and out and place on a rack in a shallow baking pan. (If you don't have a rack drain the accumulating juices after a half hour of baking.) Baste with butter. Bake 1 hour at 350° F. Baste with butter twice again during the cooking process.

Wine Sauce: From each bag of giblets select the heart and gizzard. Place these in a saucepan, cover with water and add salt. Boil for thirty minutes. Drain, cool and slice. Combine soup, gravy, pepper, sherry and sliced giblets and simmer 5 minutes. To serve: place the game hens on warmed dinner plates and ladle a spoonful of sauce over each hen. Serve remaining sauce in a gravy boat. Servings: 1 hen per person.

For other poultry recipes, see:
Chicken a la King, p. 61
Chicken Florentine, p. 64
Chicken Livers in Giblet Sauce, p. 62
Chicken Casserole, p. 63
Classic Can Can Casserole, p. 63
Ming Salad, p. 70

* * * * *

PORK, HAM AND SAUCES TO SERVE WITH BAKED HAM

Virginia's Chicken Baked Pork Chops

Here's the kind of everyday dish that families take to their hearts and adopt permanently.

4 to 6 thick pork chops
1 t salt
2 T drippings or oil
1 C instant rice
1 can (10½ oz.) cream of chicken soup
1 C milk

Using a flameproof-ovenproof covered casserole brown the salted chops in drippings. Cover with rice. Combine soup and milk, and pour over rice, making sure all rice is moistened. Cover tightly. Bake in a 350° F. oven for one hour. Serves 4.

Mexican Pork Chop Dinner

1 t salt
4 to 6 pork chops
1 envelope chili mix
1 C regular or instant rice
½ C water
1 can (1 lb.) tomatoes

Sprinkle salt in a large skillet; add chops and brown over medium heat. Sprinkle chili mix over chops, add rice, water and tomatoes. Be sure all rice is moistened. Cover, reduce heat and simmer 40 minutes. Serves 4.

Laura's Pork Tenderloin Casserole

1 can (1 lb. 12 oz.) sauerkraut
1½ lbs. pork tenderloin, cut in ½-inch slices
2 t carroway seed

Combine ingredients in a 1½-qt. covered casserole. Bake 1 hour at 350° F. If desired, brown the meat first in a little oil before adding the other ingredients. Serves 3 to 4.

Tenderloin and Stuffing Casserole

2 lbs. sliced pork tenderloin, seasoned and well browned
    (or 4 to 6 pork chops)
2 C herb-seasoned stuffing mix
1 can (8 oz.) whole kernel corn, plus liquid
1 can (1 lb.) apple slices, plus liquid
1 T frozen chopped onion
¼ C melted butter
½ t thyme

(When using pork chops remove all or most of the fat.) Place browned meat in bottom of baking dish. Cover with mixture of remaining ingredients. Cover and bake 45 minutes at 350° F. Serves 4.

Confetti Ham Casserole

2 envelopes hollandaise sauce mix
3 cans (15 oz. each) macaroni and cheese
2 C cooked ham, slivered
1 jar (2 oz.) pimiento, drained and chopped
¾ C frozen chopped green pepper
½ t prepared mustard
¼ C sherry
¼ C grated Cheddar cheese

In a chafing dish or serving dish-skillet prepare hollandaise sauce as directed. Add macaroni and cheese, ham, pimiento, green pepper and mustard. Simmer 20 minutes. Add sherry, sprinkle with grated cheese. Heat 5 more minutes. (Or combine all ingredients and bake 30 minutes at 350° F.) Serves 6.

Romanoff Dinner

Here's a wonderful blend of made-for-each-other flavors.

1 pkg. noodles Romanoff mix
1½ C cooked ham, cut in strips
1 can (8 oz.) cut green beans

Prepare noodle mix as directed, but increase milk to 2/3 C. Add ham and beans. Bake in a 1½-qt. covered casserole 20 minutes at 350° F. Serves 3 to 4.

Caribbean Ham Dinner

1 2-lb. ham slice, 1¼ inches thick
1 can (1 lb.) pineapple chunks, plus juice
½ C maple syrup
1 t allspice
¼ t pepper
1 can (29 oz.) sweet potatoes or yams

Score fat that rings ham. Sear in a heavy serving dish-skillet. Combine pineapple chunks, juice, maple syrup, all-spice and pepper and pour over ham. Cover and simmer 30 minutes or until ham is cooked and tender. During last 10 minutes of cooking place sweet potatoes around ham and baste with juices. Serve in skillet when potatoes are heated through. Serves 4.

Glazed Ham Steak

1 or 2 ham steaks, 1·inch thick
1 can (12 oz.) apricot nectar
2 t Worcestershire sauce
2 T brown sugar

Score fat edges of ham steaks. Place in a shallow baking pan. Combine remaining ingredients and pour half of mixture over ham. Bake 45 minutes at 350° F. Baste occasionally with remaining sauce. Serve with pan drippings. Allow ½ lb. per person.

SAUCES TO SERVE WITH BAKED HAM

HOT SAUCES

Raisin Sauce

1 envelope brown gravy mix (or beef gravy mix)
1 C apple juice
2 T raisins

Dissolve gravy mix in apple juice, add raisins. Bring mixture to a boil stirring constantly. Reduce heat and simmer 5 minutes. Makes 1 cup.

Madeira Sauce

2 cans (10¾ oz. each) brown gravy
¼ C madeira wine

Combine and heat to boiling. Makes about 3 cups. Use this with beef, too.

Orange Sauce

1 envelope brown or beef gravy mix
½ C water
½ C orange juice
1 t Worcestershire sauce
1 t sugar

Combine ingredients and heat to boiling. Stir constantly.
Makes 1 cup. Good with game, too.

Curry Sauce

1 can (10½ oz.) cream of celery soup
1/3 C milk
½ t curry powder

Combine ingredients and heat to boiling. Stir constantly.
Makes about 2 cups. This is good with fish, too.

COLD SAUCES

Dill Sauce

1 large garlic dill pickle, cut up
½ C sour cream
¼ t dill weed
¼ t salt

Place all ingredients in blender and process until smooth.
Makes about 1 cup. Also good with cooked or raw vegetables.

Mustard Sauce

1 C mayonnaise
1/3 C horseradish-style mustard

Stir mustard into mayonnaise until completely blended.
Makes 1 1/3 cups. Try this with seafood or broiled sausages.

* * * * *

VEAL, LAMB AND CHOP SUEY

Veal Scallopine, Sorrento Style

1 lb. veal slices
Flour
¼ C oil
1 jar (1 lb.) marinara or spaghetti sauce
¼ lb. mozzarella cheese, cut in 12 slices
1 can (2 oz.) flat anchovy fillets
¼ C grated Parmesan cheese

Ask the butcher to cut veal Italian style in 12 pieces; or have veal cut in thin slices and pound to ¼-inch thickness. Flour the meat lightly and brown quickly in oil. Spread half the marinara sauce in a large shallow baking dish. Arrange veal on sauce. Cover with remaining sauce, place 1 piece of cheese over each piece of meat, and top with an anchovy fillet. Sprinkle with Parmesan cheese and bake 12 minutes at 450° F. Serves 3 to 4.

Veal Cordon Bleu—American Style

8 veal slices, pounded thin (1½ lbs.)
4 slices boiled ham
4 slices American cheese (also try Swiss or mozarella)
½ C potato flakes
¼ C butter
1 t salt

Cut ham and cheese slices in half. Place a half slice of each on each veal slice. Roll up and secure with toothpick. Melt butter in shallow baking dish. Coat meat rolls with butter, roll in potato flakes and salt, and arrange in shallow baking dish. Bake 20 minutes in a 400° F. oven or until brown. Or, sauté in butter until brown, 10 minutes on each side. Serves 4 to 6.

Lamb Curry #1

1/3 C raisins
½ C water
1 can (10½ oz.) cream of chicken soup
½ t curry powder
2 C leftover lamb, cut in ¾-inch pieces
½ C salted peanuts

Simmer raisins in water 5 minutes. Stir in remaining ingredients and heat through. Serve on hot rice, garnish with salted peanuts. Serves 2 or 3.

Lamb Curry #2

½ C frozen chopped onion
½ C frozen chopped green pepper
2 T oil
1 can (10½ oz.) golden mushroom soup
1/3 C milk
½ t curry powder
1 jar (8 oz.) chopped pears (junior foods)
1 can (4 oz.) whole mushrooms
2 C cooked lamb, cut in bite-size pieces

Sauté onion and pepper in oil until just tender; add remaining ingredients. Cover and heat through. Serve with rice and chutney. Serves 2 to 3.

Veal In Sour Cream

3 lbs. veal, cut in 1-inch cubes
1 can (4½ oz.) sliced mushrooms
1 can (10½ oz.) cream of mushroom soup
1 envelope onion soup mix
1 C water
½ C sauterne or other white wine
½ t Italian seasoning
1 C sour cream

40

Mix all ingredients except sour cream in a heavy casserole. Cover and bake 2 hours at 325° F. Stir in sour cream just before serving. (Do not allow the sauce to come to a boil after sour cream has been added.) Serves 8.

Veal Gourmet

1½ lbs. veal, cut from the round
1 egg, slightly beaten with 2 T water
½ C bread crumbs
Paprika
1 t salt
¼ C butter
1 can (10½ oz.) cream of chicken soup
¾ C half-and-half cream
1 can (1 lb.) pitted Queen Anne cherries, plus ¼ C juice

Have veal cut in 1½-inch pieces. Dip veal in egg mixture, coat with crumbs and sprinkle with paprika and salt. Sauté in butter until brown. Stir in soup, cream and cherry juice. Simmer on lowest heat for 45 minutes. Add drained cherries during last 5 minutes. Serves 4.

Shish Kabob

Marinate lamb using ingredients in *Lamb en Brochette*. When ready to cook, alternate the following ingredients with the lamb on the skewers:

3 lge. green peppers, cut in 2-inch squares
1 can (16 oz.) whole onions
1 lb. large mushrooms
16 to 32 plum or cherry tomatoes

Brush assembled kabobs with remaining marinade and broil approximately 10 minutes. Serves 8.

Lamb en Brochette

3 to 4 lbs. lamb, cut in 1½-inch cubes
3 T reconstituted lemon juice
6 T soy sauce
4 T olive or salad oil
¼ t pepper
½ C bottled onion juice (or 1 large grated onion)

Combine all ingredients and allow meat to marinate at least
an hour. Turn the meat in the mixture occasionally.
Thread the meat cubes on skewers and broil. Serves 8.

Italian Veal Con Riso

6 (1¼ lbs.) pre-breaded veal cutlets
¼ lb. Italian sausage, sliced
¼ C oil
2 C cooked rice
1 can (10½ oz.) minestrone soup
1 soup can water
2 cans (4 oz. each) tomato paste
¼ C grated Parmesan cheese
2 T instant minced onion
2 T dry parsley flakes

In a fancy skillet, brown and cook veal and sausage in oil
until done. Transfer to a paper plate temporarily. Combine
remaining ingredients, stirring to blend. Tuck veal pieces
into this mixture. Decorate each cutlet with a sausage slice.
Cover and heat 5 more minutes. Serves 4.

Mint Sauce For Roast Lamb

½ C mint-flavored apple jelly
2 T butter

Combine and heat until melted and blended. Baste lamb
roast during last half hour of roasting or serve as a warm
sauce at the table. (Or double the recipe and do both.)

Chop Suey

1 lb. chop suey meat (1-inch pieces veal, pork and beef)
1 T oil
1 envelope onion soup mix
2 t soy sauce
2 C water
2 C celery, sliced on the diagonal ¼ inch thick
1 can (16 oz.) chop suey vegetables
2 T cornstarch

Brown meat in oil. Add soup mix, soy sauce and water; simmer 30 minutes or until meat is done. Add celery and vegetables, heat through. (Celery should remain crunchy and green.) Dissolve cornstarch in ¼ C water, stir into chop suey. Heat and stir until mixture thickens and becomes clear. Serves 3.

Chow Mein

1 can (10¾ oz.) brown gravy
1 t soy sauce
1 can (16 oz.) chop suey vegetables
1 or 2 C leftover veal, pork or beef, cut in cubes
1 can (3 oz.) chow mein noodles

Combine all ingredients except noodles and heat thoroughly. Serve over chow mein noodles. Serves 2 to 4.

For additional chop suey recipes, see:
Pineapple Chicken Chow Mein, p. 32

* * * * *

FISH AND SHELLFISH

Fish and Fries Platter

1 lb. frozen fish sticks or breaded fillets
½ C tartar sauce (bottled or use recipe below)
1 pkg. (10 to 12 oz.) French fries or potato puffs
1 pkg. (9 oz.) French fried onion rings
1 pkg. (7 oz.) French fried clams

Spread fish sticks with tartar sauce. Arrange fish and potatoes on a large metal platter or baking sheet and bake at
400° F. for 10 minutes. Add onion rings and clams to
platter and continue baking another 10 minutes. Serves 4.

Shrimp Almondine in Noodle Nests

1 pkg. (10 oz.) frozen peas in butter sauce
1 can (10 oz.) frozen cream of shrimp soup, thawed
½ C sour cream
⅛ t saffron
1 lb. frozen shrimp, cooked
¼ C slivered almonds, toasted
4 chow mein noodle nests (or 3 C hot cooked rice)

Prepare peas as directed. Drain butter sauce into a chafing
dish and add soup, sour cream and saffron. Blend. Add
peas, shrimp and almonds. Heat through. Spoon into
heated noodle nests or serve with rice. Serves 4.

Seafood Vol au Vent

1 pkg. (10 oz.) frozen puff pastry shells (6 shells)
2 pkgs. frozen lobster Newberg (11½ oz. each.)
¼ C sherry

Bake shells as directed; cool. Heat lobster Newberg as directed, add sherry before serving. Fill shells with lobster
mixture. Serves 3 non-dieters.

Baked Fillet of Sole

Remember when the sauce element in every easy casserole was cream of mushroom soup? It was, and still is, a magic ingredient. But competitors for its unique position in the cooking world have appeared at last. One of the newest no-work sauces on the scene is frozen cream of shrimp soup. Pretty-pink and full of tiny whole shrimp it has no equal in quick fish and seafood dishes.

1 lb. frozen fillet of sole, thawed
1 can (10 oz.) frozen cream of shrimp soup, thawed
½ C (about) grated Parmesan cheese
1½ T butter

Place sole (thawed and patted dry on paper towels) in a shallow baking dish and cover with soup. Sprinkle with cheese, dot with butter, and bake 30 minutes at 375° F. Serves 3.

Florentine Salmon Steaks

1 envelope sour cream sauce mix
½ C milk
¼ C mayonnaise
2 pkgs. (10 oz. each) frozen chopped spinach, thawed
½ t salt
1 T butter
4 salmon steaks, fresh or frozen
¼ C buttered bread crumbs

Stir milk into sauce mix until smooth; let stand 10 minutes. Blend mayonnaise into sauce mixture. Spread thawed, uncooked spinach in bottom of greased, shallow baking dish. Sprinkle with salt, dot with butter, and place salmon steaks over spinach. Spread salmon with sour cream mixture and top with bread crumbs. Bake in a 350° F. oven for 30 minutes or until salmon is done. Serves 4.

Ruth's Something Special Salmon

1 pkg. (9 oz.) frozen artichoke hearts, cooked as directed
1 can (1 lb.) red salmon
1 lemon, sliced *very* thin
2 T capers
1 C sour cream
Buttered bread crumbs

Place artichoke hearts in a 1-qt. casserole. Follow with 1 layer each of salmon, lemon slices (reserve a few slices for garnish), capers and sour cream. Top with buttered crumbs. Bake at 350° F. for 30 minutes. Crumbs should brown. (To prepare buttered crumbs melt 2 T butter in a skillet, add ½ C prepared bread crumbs. Stir to mix.) Serves 2 or 3.

Tuna Casserole Supreme

1 pkg. macaroni and cheese dinner
1 can (7 oz.) tuna, flaked
1 can (3 oz.) sliced mushrooms
½ C sour cream
¼ C milk
2 T frozen chopped onion
¼ t celery salt
⅛ t fresh ground pepper

Prepare macaroni dinner as directed; add remaining ingredients. Bake in a 1-qt. casserole for 20 minutes at 350° F. Serves 3.

Baked Shrimp

Follow recipe for Baked Fillet of Sole, p. 45; but substitute 1 lb. frozen cleaned, shelled shrimp for the sole fillets. The shrimp need not be thawed, but be sure to remove any excess ice. Serves 3.

Crabmeat Gourmet

2 cans (10 oz. each) frozen cream of shrimp soup, thawed
1 (13 oz.) can lobster soup (non-condensed type)
1 C half-and-half cream
2 egg yolks, beaten
¼ C sherry
1½ lbs. frozen crabmeat, thawed
1 pkg. brown and wild rice, prepared as directed

Combine and heat soups, cream and egg yolks. Stir in crabmeat and sherry. Heat to bubbling and transfer to a chafing dish. Serve over brown and wild rice. Serves 6 to 8.

Rice-bed Shrimp

3 C hot cooked rice
2 cans (4½ oz. each) shrimp
1 C sour cream
3 oz. blue cheese, crumbled
1 t Worcestershire sauce

Spoon rice into 4 (1½ C capacity) ramekins. Arrange shrimp on rice. Combine sour cream, cheese and Worcestershire sauce; spoon over shrimp. Cover and bake 15 minutes at 350° F. Serves 4 lightly.

Lynn's Cashew Casserole

1 can (10½ oz.) cream of mushroom soup
1 can (7 oz.) tuna
1 can (3 oz.) chow mein noodles
¼ lb. cashews, salted or plain
½ C diced celery
¼ C frozen minced onion

Combine all ingredients and bake in an ovenproof dish for 40 minutes at 325° F. Serves 3.

Fish Stick Casserole

2 pkgs. (10 oz. each) frozen mixed vegetables with onion
    sauce
1 t Worcestershire sauce
3 med. tomatoes, sliced ½ inch thick
1 pkg. (16 oz.) fish sticks
6 strips bacon

Here's wonderful color and flavor. Prepare vegetables as
directed, adding Worcestershire sauce to onion sauce. Pour
into a shallow baking dish (8 x 12 inches), cover with tomato slices and top with fish sticks. Sprinkle with additional Worcestershire sauce, if desired. Cover with bacon
strips and bake 20 minutes at 375° F. Serves 4.

Salmon Romanoff Casserole

1 pkg. sour cream-cheese sauce and noodle mix
1 can (8 oz.) salmon
½ C cottage cheese
2 T frozen chives

Prepare noodles and sauce mix as directed, but increase
milk to 2/3 C. Stir in salmon, cheese and chives. Bake in
a 1-qt. covered casserole, 20 minutes at 350° F. Serves 2
to 3.

Shrimp Egg Foo Young

1 pkg. (14 oz.) egg foo young mix
1 can (4½ oz.) shrimp, diced
1 t soy sauce

Prepare egg foo young mix as directed, adding diced
shrimp and soy sauce to egg and vegetable mixture. Cook
as directed. To serve, arrange patties on a hot platter and
pour sauce included in mix over all. Serve with rice.
Serves 2.

Fish Sticks in Cheese Sauce

8 to 12 oz. frozen fish sticks or breaded fillets
1 envelope cheese sauce mix, prepared as directed
½ t parsley flakes
1 t lemon juice

Arrange fish sticks in a shallow baking dish. Combine prepared cheese sauce, parsley and lemon juice. Pour over fish and bake 25 minutes at 350° F. Serves 2.

Baked Scallops

1 lb. scallops (cut large scallops in 1-inch pieces)
1 pkg. (2 oz.) seasoned coating mix for fish

Moisten scallops with water or milk and coat wtih seasoned coating mix. Arrange scallops on a greased baking sheet. Bake at 400° F. for 15 minutes. Serve with Seafood Cocktail Sauce (below). Serve 2 to 3.

Scallops in Shrimp Sauce

Follow recipe for Baked Fillet of Sole p. 45 substituting 1 lb. scallops for sole. (Cut large scallops in 1-inch pieces.) Serves 3.

SEAFOOD SAUCES

Seafood Cocktail Sauce

1 C ketchup
2 T horseradish

Combine ingredients and serve cold. Makes 1 generous cup.

Tartar Sauce

½ C mayonnaise
2 T sweet pickle relish

Combine and serve. Makes ½ cup.

For additional fish and shellfish recipes, see:
Red Clam Sauce for Spaghetti, p. 52
Crabmeat Spaghetti Sauce, p. 53
Shell Salad with Shrimp, p. 70
Spaghetti with Shrimp, p. 53
Shrimp Artichoke Salad, p. 70
Paella (with lobster, shrimp and clams), p. 55

* * * * *

SPAGHETTI SAUCES
AND LASAGNA

Note: Good tasting, single-stranded pasta is yours for a lump of butter. Add a tablespoon or two of butter to each half pound of hot spaghetti in its serving dish. Toss quickly to melt. And don't forget, the best pasta is never over-cooked.

Spaghetti Romanoff

1 jar (1 lb.) spaghetti sauce (meat, meatless or mushroom)
1 pkg. (3 oz.) cream cheese, softened
½ C water
½ lb. spaghetti, cooked according to directions

Gradually add spaghetti sauce to softened cream cheese, mixing until well blended. Add water and heat. Serve with cooked spaghetti. Serves 3.

Mr. X's Favorite Italian Spaghetti Sauce

1 lb. ground round steak
1 t seasoned salt
1 lb. Italian sausage (hot or sweet)
2 t oil
1½ C frozen chopped green pepper
1½ C frozen chopped onion
1 can (29 oz.) tomatoes
1 can (15 oz.) tomato sauce
1 envelope spaghetti sauce mix
¼ C grated Parmesan cheese

Combine ground round steak and seasoned salt and shape into small balls 1½ inches in diameter; slice sausage in 1-inch pieces. Brown both in oil in a large 3- or 4-qt. frying pan. Push aside and sauté green pepper and onion 8 minutes. Remove excess fat. Add remaining ingredients and simmer, covered, 2 hours. Serves 6 to 8.

Lasagna

2 jars (1 lb. each) spaghetti sauce with meat
½ C water
1 lb. ricotta cheese (or dry cottage cheese)
1 egg
¾ C grated Romano and Parmesan cheese
½ lb. ribbed lasagna noodles, cooked
1 lb. mozzarella cheese, sliced

Blend sauce and water; heat. Beat together ricotta, egg and 2 T grated cheese. Spread a thin layer of sauce on bottom of 9 x 13-inch baking pan; arrange layer of noodles, spread with ricotta mixture. Top with a layer of mozzarella, another layer of sauce and a sprinkling of grated cheese. Repeat these layers until all ingredients are used, ending with a layer of sauce and a layer of grated cheese. Bake 30 minutes at 350° F. Serves 8.

Spaghetti Sauce with Wine

¼ C dried imported mushrooms
½ C water
2 lbs. ground beef
2 t seasoned salt
2 envelopes spaghetti sauce mix, prepared as directed
1 jar (4 oz.) sliced mushrooms, plus juice
½ C red wine

Hydrate dried mushrooms in water for half an hour. Add seasoned salt to ground beef and brown in a large skillet. Prepare spaghetti sauce mix in the same pan and add both kinds of mushrooms and the water. Add the wine and simmer 45 minutes. Serve with 1 lb. spaghetti, cooked, and Parmesan cheese. Serves 8.

Sicilian Spaghetti

1 pkg. spaghetti with meat sauce mix
1 can (4½ oz.) chopped ripe olives
Parmesan cheese

Prepare spaghetti as directed on package. Add olives to sauce and heat; pour over cooked spaghetti and sprinkle with Parmesan cheese. Serves 2 to 3.

Red Clam Sauce For Spaghetti

1 envelope spaghetti sauce mix
1 can (1 lb.) tomatoes
1 can (1 lb.) tomato sauce
2 cans (7½ oz. each) minced clams (plus juice)
½ lb. spaghetti, cooked according to directions

Combine spaghetti sauce mix, tomatoes, tomato sauce and clam juice. Simmer 30 minutes. Add clams, heat through and serve on cooked spaghetti. Serves 3 to 4.

Spaghetti With Shrimp

1 to 1½ lbs. cleaned frozen shrimp
2 garlic cloves, chopped
¼ t oregano
¼ C oil
1 envelope spaghetti sauce mix, prepared as directed
Pinch red pepper seeds
½ lb. spaghetti, cooked according to directions

Cut up shrimp, and sauté in oil with garlic and oregano until tender (about 5 minutes). Add pinch of red pepper seeds to prepared spaghetti sauce. Combine shrimp and sauce just before serving. Toss with cooked spaghetti. Serves 4.

Instant Spaghetti and Meatballs

1 or 2 cans (1 lb. each) spaghetti sauce
1 can (1 lb.) meatballs and gravy
1 can (4 oz.) whole button mushrooms
½ t garlic salt

Combine all ingredients and heat to bubbling. Serve with ½ lb. cooked spaghetti. Toss spaghetti with 2 T butter and ¼ C grated Parmesan cheese. Serves 3.

Ravioli Casserole (Mock Lasagna)

1 can (2½ lb.) ravioli
½ pt. cottage cheese
½ lb. mozzarella (or scamorza) cheese, sliced
1 can (8 oz.) pizza sauce
½ C grated Parmesan cheese

In a 9-inch square baking pan, arrange in layers half portions of ingredients in order given. Repeat layers with remaining portions. Bake 30 minutes at 350° F. Serves 4 to 6.

Crabmeat Spaghetti Sauce

2 pkgs. frozen crabmeat (6 oz. each) or 2 (7 oz.) cans
2 cans (10 oz. each) cream of celery soup
¼ C dried parsley flakes
¼ C sliced ripe olives
2 T frozen minced onion
1 t Worcestershire sauce

Combine frozen crabmeat and remaining ingredients in saucepan. Cover tightly and simmer 15 minutes, stirring occasionally. Serve with ½ lb. spaghetti, cooked. When using canned crabmeat, reduce simmer time to 5 minutes. Serves 4.

For additional spaghetti recipes, see:
Chicken Tetrazzini, p. 31
Stuffed Peppers, Italian Style, p. 63
Sara's Welcome Neighbor Casserole, p. 23
Chicken Cacciatore, p. 26

* * * * *

CHILI AND SOUTH OF THE BORDER DISHES

Note: Chili dishes cooked on top of the stove must be heated slowly to prevent burning, but the hurried homemaker often has little patience with instructions to go slowly. To speed up the heating process turn the stove burner on high and start stirring. Don't walk away! Stir constantly until the mixture starts to bubble, then turn the heat down to simmer. (On an electric stove continue to stir for a minute while the coil temperature is reducing.) If you can't resist the temptation to answer the telephone while the heat is on high forget this method—you'll surely burn the chili!

Paella

1 pkg. (1 lb.) frozen rock lobster tails (small)
2 cans (1 lb. 12 oz. each) tomatoes
2 cans (7½ oz. each) minced clams, plus juice
2 envelopes Spanish rice seasoning mix
2 garlic cloves, crushed
¼ t saffron
1 T MSG
3 C instant rice
1 pkg. (24 oz.) frozen cleaned shrimp
1 pkg. (9 oz.) frozen artichoke hearts
2 C frozen peas
2 C cooked boned chicken
½ C stuffed olives

Cook lobster tails according to package directions. Cut underside membrane but do not remove meat; set aside. Pour tomatoes and clams into a 16-inch paella pan and begin to heat. If the tomatoes are large, cut them up a bit. Stir in seasoning mix, garlic, saffron and MSG. Add remaining ingredients and bring to a boil. Garnish with lobster tails, cover with foil and simmer 15 minutes. Serves 10 to 12. Serve with Sangria, p. 181.

Corncake Chili Dinner

1 pkg. (9 oz.) corn muffin mix
1 egg
1½ C milk
½ C whole kernel corn, drained
3 cans chili (1 lb. each)
½ C shredded Cheddar cheese

Combine corn muffin mix, egg, milk, and corn. Stir just until dry ingredients are moistened. Divide into 12 pancakes and fry on a hot griddle. Heat chili. Spoon ¼ C chili on each pancake and fold pancake in half. Place folded, filled pancakes on heated platter, pour remaining chili over pancakes and sprinkle with cheese. Serves 6.

Chili Chip Casserole

1 lb. ground beef
1 C frozen chopped onion
1 envelope chili seasoning mix
1 can (6 oz.) tomato paste
¾ C water
1 bag (6 oz.) corn chips
1 can (1 lb.) pinto or kidney beans
1 can (4½ oz.) sliced or chopped ripe olives
2 C grated Cheddar cheese (½ lb.)

Brown the beef, add onion, chili mix, tomato paste, and water. Simmer 10 minutes. Sprinkle 2 C (½ bag) corn chips in bottom of 2½-qt. casserole. Spoon half the meat mixture over it, followed by a layer of half the beans, half the olives, and 1 C cheese. Repeat all layers except corn chips. Sprinkle remaining corn chips over all. Cover and bake 30 min. at 350° F. Remove cover and bake an additional 15 minutes. Serves 4 to 6.

Deep Dish Chili Pie

1 lb. ground beef
1 t salt
1 can (6 oz.) tomato paste
2 C water
1 can (1 lb.) whole kernel corn
1 C grated Cheddar cheese
1 can (4½ oz.) chopped ripe olives
1 envelope chili seasoning mix
1 pkg. (8½ oz.) corn muffin mix, prepared as directed

Brown the ground beef and combine with remaining ingredients, except corn muffin mix, in a 2½-qt. casserole. Bake at 400° F. for 20 minutes. Spoon prepared corn muffin mix over the hot meat mixture. Return to oven and continue baking 15 minutes. Serves 6.

Chili Shortcake

1 green pepper, cut in strips
1 pkg. (9 oz.) corn muffin mix
2 cans (1 lb. each) beef chili with beans

Place half the green pepper strips in the bottom of a greased 8-inch square cake pan. Prepare corn muffin mix as directed and pour over pepper strips. Bake as directed. Cool. Heat chili. Slice cornbread in two layers, spoon half of hot chili on bottom layer, cover with second layer. Spoon remaining chili on top layer and garnish with remaining strips of green pepper. Serves 3 to 4.

Meatball Chili

1 envelope chili seasoning mix
1 can (1 lb.) tomatoes
½ C water
1 can (1 lb.) meatballs and gravy
½ lb egg noodles, cooked as directed
3 T butter

Combine all but noodles and butter and simmer for 10 minutes. Drain noodles, add butter. Stir gently over low heat to melt butter and coat noodles. Serve wih meatball mixture. Serves 2.

Chili Beef Stew

2 cans (1½ lbs. each) beef stew
1 envelope chili seasoning mix
2 t vinegar

Combine and heat. Serve with 1½ C instant rice prepared as directed. Serves 4.

Tamale Casserole

3 C corn chips
1 can tamales
1 C frozen chopped onion
1 can (1 lb.) chili
1 C grated Cheddar cheese (¼ lb.)

Place 2 cups of the corn chips in the bottom of a 2-qt. casserole. Arrange tamales on top of the chips and cover with the chopped onion. Pour the can of chili over all and top with the remaining cup of corn chips and the grated cheese. Bake uncovered at 350° F. for 25 minutes. Serves 3.

Bean Dip Chili

1½ lbs. ground beef
1 can (1 lb.) tomatoes
½ C water
1 envelope chili seasoning mix
1 (7½ oz.) can bean dip

Brown the beef and stir in remaining ingredients. Simmer five to ten minutes. (Be sure to remove excess fat after the meat has browned before adding the other ingredients.) Serves 4. Bean Dip Chili can also be used as a hot dip. Serve it with corn chips.

Chiliburgers

1 C frozen chopped onion
1 lb. ground beef
1 can (16 oz.) tomato sauce
1 t salt
¼ t pepper
1 can (12 oz.) whole kernel corn
Pinch chili powder

Brown beef and onions, add remaining ingredients. Simmer 30 minutes. Serve on toasted hamburger buns. Serves 6.

Chili and Rice

1 lb. ground beef
1 T oil
1 envelope chili mix
1 1/3 C instant rice
1 can (6 oz.) tomato paste
3 C hot water

Brown beef in oil. Stir in chili mix. Add instant rice, tomato paste and hot water. Bring to a boil. Reduce heat and simmer 10 minutes. Serves 3 to 4.

Onion Soup Chili

1½ lbs. ground beef
1 envelope onion soup mix
1 t to 2 T chili powder, according to taste
2 cans (1 lb. each) kidney beans
½ C water
1 can (1 lb.) tomatoes

Brown the beef in a large skillet and stir in the remaining ingredients. Cover and simmer 30 to 40 minutes. Serves 6.

Chili Stew

1 can (1 lb.) tomatoes
1 can (1 lb.) small whole potatoes
1 can (1 lb.) cream-style corn
1 can (1 lb.) kidney beans
1 or 2 cans (1 lb. each) meatballs and gravy
1 envelope chili seasoning mix

Combine all ingredients and heat slowly in a 3-qt. saucepan. Or, combine ingredients in a 3-qt. casserole and bake 30 minutes at 350° F. Serves 6.

Enchilada Casserole

1 pkg. (22 oz.) frozen beef enchiladas
1 lb. ground beef
1 can (1 lb.) tomatoes
1 can (1 lb.) pinto or kidney beans
1 envelope chili seasoning mix
½ C grated Cheddar cheese, optional

Remove frozen enchiladas from baking container (they slip out easily) and place cheese side up in an 8 x 12-inch baking dish. Brown ground beef and combine with tomatoes, beans and chili mix. Heat to a boil and spoon around the enchiladas in the baking dish. Sprinkle on the cheese if desired. Cover with foil and bake 40 minutes at 350° F. If enchiladas are allowed to thaw (in the refrigerator) before adding chili mixture, reduce baking time to 20 minutes. Serves 4.

For additional South of the Border recipes, see:
Tacos, p. 69
Chihuahuas, p. 68
Hot Taco Dogs, p. 67
Arroz con Pollo, p. 27

Luncheon and Supper Entrees

Generally, luncheon and supper entrees are lighter fare than the recipes for meats and main dishes. A good many of them, however, will do double duty as a main dish for dinner.

Other luncheon and supper ideas may be found in the Breakfast and Brunch chapter and in the Fish, Chili, and Chicken sections of Meats and Main Dishes. Especially recommended for luncheon parties are the shellfish recipes in the Fish section.

* * * * *

FOR THE CHAFING DISH

Chicken a la King

1 pkg. frozen mushrooms and butter, prepared as directed
2 cans (10½ oz. each) chicken a la king
2 T dry white wine
1 T frozen chopped chives
4 frozen waffles, heated and buttered

Add chicken a la king to hot prepared mushrooms in a chafing dish. Stir in wine and chives and heat through. To serve: spoon hot chicken mixture over warm buttered waffles. Serves 4.

61

Chicken Livers in Giblet Sauce

1 lb. chicken livers
3 T butter
1 jar (4 oz.) sliced mushrooms
Salt and pepper to taste
1 can (10½ oz.) giblet gravy
1 can (10½ oz.) mushroom gravy
¼ C vermouth (or dry sherry)

Sauté livers in butter 10 minutes. Add mushrooms during the last few minutes. Salt and pepper lightly. In a chafing dish combine and heat gravies and wine; simmer 5 minutes. Add chicken livers and mushrooms. Serve over hot buttered rice (approximately 3 C cooked rice to which 1 t parsley flakes have been added.) Serves 4.

* * * * *

CASEROLES

Stuffed Peppers

4 to 6 medium green peppers
½ C instant rice, cooked as directed
1 can (1 lb.) tomatoes
1 envelope brown gravy mix
1½ to 2 C diced cooked beef
Seasoned pepper

Remove tops, seeds and white membrane from peppers. Boil in salted water 5 minutes. To the cooked rice add tomatoes, and gravy mix. Heat. Place peppers upright in an ovenproof serving dish. Add meat to the rice mixture, and stuff the peppers with this mixture. Sprinkle tops with seasoned pepper. Bake 20 to 30 minutes at 350° F. Leftover lamb, veal, pork, or turkey may be used in place of beef. Serves 4.

Stuffed Peppers, Italian Style

4 to 6 medium green peppers
1 pkg. spaghetti with meat sauce mix, prepared as directed
1/3 C Italian bread crumbs
1/3 C Parmesan cheese

Remove tops and seeds from peppers; parboil 5 minutes. Combine spaghetti and meat sauce. Stuff peppers with mixture and place in a greased baking dish. Sprinkle tops with mixture of cheese and crumbs. Bake at 350° F. for 20 minutes. Serves 4.

Classic Can Can Casserole

1 large can (5 oz.) chow mein noodles
1 jar (1 lb.) boned chicken, tuna, crabmeat or shrimp
1 can (10½ oz.) cream of chicken soup
1 can (10½ oz.) chicken rice soup
1 can (4 oz.) sliced mushrooms
¼ C milk
1 T butter

Reserve ½ C noodles (coarsely crushed) for top of casserole. Combine chicken, soups, mushrooms, milk, and remaining noodles in a 2-qt. ovenproof serving dish. Top with crushed noodles, dot with butter. Bake 30 minutes at 350° F. Serves 6.

Chicken Stuffing Casserole

2 C herb-seasoned stuffing mix, prepared as directed
2 cans (7 oz.) boned chicken (or 1½ to 2 C leftover
    chicken)
1 can (10½ oz.) cream of chicken soup
8 sliced stuffed olives
¼ t poultry seasoning

Place half of prepared stuffing in 1½- to 2-qt. ovenproof serving dish. Combine chicken, soup, olives and seasoning and pour over stuffing. Top with remaining stuffing and bake, uncovered, 20 to 30 minutes at 350° F. Serves 3.

Chicken Florentine

2 pkgs. (10 oz. each) frozen chopped spinach, thawed
Salt, pepper and nutmeg
6 eggs
2 pkgs. (10 to 12 oz. each) frozen escalloped chicken and
    noodles or chicken a la king, partly thawed
¼ C grated Parmesan cheese

Squeeze excess moisture from spinach. Divide equally in 6
(8 oz.) ramekins. Sprinkle with salt, pepper and nutmeg.
Drop 1 raw egg in each dish. Spoon chicken mixture over
egg and sprinkle with cheese. Bake 25 minutes at 350° F.
Serves 6.

* * * * *

PIZZAS

Shrimp Pizza

1 pkg. complete cheese pizza mix
2 T prepared mustard
1 can (6 oz.) shrimp

Make up pizza dough according to package directions.
Cover crust with mustard, arrange shrimp over mustard,
and cover with pizza sauce. Sprinkle grated cheese over
all and bake as directed. Serves 4.

Mama's Pizza

1 pkg. hot roll mix, prepared as directed for pizza dough
Oil
1 can (16 oz.) pizza sauce
1 lb. scamorza or mozzarella cheese, grated or sliced thin
1 pkg. (¾ lb.) smoky link sausages, sliced ¼ inch thick
1 t oregano

Roll out two rounds of dough to fit two oiled pizza pans or roll out two rectangles to fit cookie sheets. Brush dough lightly with oil and spread 1 C pizza sauce on each piece. Arrange sausage slices and cheese evenly over sauce and sprinkle with oregano. Bake one at a time 10 minutes at 500° F. Serves 8. (Freeze one unbaked pizza if two is too many. Just wrap securely in foil or tuck pan into a large plastic bag and seal.)

* * * * *

SOUFFLÉS

Danish Soufflé

12 slices slightly dry white bread (trim crusts)
½ lb. shredded sharp Cheddar cheese
1/3 C imitation bacon bits (or 6 slices bacon cooked and
    crumbled)
3 T frozen chives
4 eggs
2½ C milk
1 t salt
1/8 t pepper

Place 6 slices of bread in bottom of oiled 8x12x2-inch baking pan. Sprinkle with half the cheese, bacon bits and chives. Cover with remaining 6 bread slices and distribute remaining cheese, bacon bits and chives on top. Beat together last four ingredients and pour over bread slices. Let stand at least 30 minutes before baking at 325° F. for 50 minutes. Serves 6.

Cheese Soufflé

1 can (10¾ oz.) Cheddar cheese soup
6 eggs, separated
2 pkgs. (8 oz. each) frozen mixed vegetables in onion
     sauce, prepared as directed

Heat soup, stirring constantly. Remove from heat and set
aside. Beat egg yolks until thick and stir into slightly
cooled soup. Beat egg whites until stiff; fold soup mixture
into egg whites. Pour into a 2½-qt. casserole and bake 35
minutes at 325° F. and 10 minutes more at 350° F. To
serve: spoon cooked vegetables in onion sauce over each
soufflé serving. Serves 6.

* * * * *

SANDWICHES

Delicatessen Special

6 onion rolls
1½ lbs. kosher corned beef, thinly sliced, from the
     delicatessen
Prepared mustard

Split onion rolls. Place a ½-inch layer of corned beef on
bottom half of bun. Spread mustard on top half and place
on corned beef. Wrap securely in squares of aluminum
foil and heat in a 350° F. oven, 12 to 15 minutes. 6 servings.

Crescent Surprises

1 can refrigerator crescent rolls
1 can (1 lb.) asparagus spears
2 slices American cheese, cut in quarters
4 slices ham, cut in half

Unfold 8 crescent rolls. Place cheese, ham and one asparagus spear on each piece of dough. Roll up and spear with
toothpick. Bake 20 minutes at 375° F. Serves 4.

Boo's Hot Crabmeat Special

1 can crabmeat
½ lb. processed American cheese
2 dashes garlic salt
¼ C butter or margarine
4 English muffins, split

Combine and heat first four ingredients in top of double boiler. Spread on muffin halves. Broil until brown. (Careful! It takes just a minute.) Serve with a fruit salad or tossed vegetable salad at a ladies' luncheon. Serves 4.

Pizzaburgers

1½ lb. ground beef
1 t salt
½ C pizza-flavored catsup
1 T frozen chopped onion
6 slices mozzarella cheese
3 split, buttered and toasted buns

Combine meat, salt, ¼ C catsup, and onion; shape in 6 patties. Fry or broil until done, about 5 minutes on each side. Spread 1 T-pizza flavored catsup on each bun half, top with patty and a slice of cheese. Place under broiler just long enough to melt cheese slightly. 6 servings.

Tangy Sloppy Joes

1 lb. ground beef
1 C ketchup
½ C pickle relish
1 t seasoned salt
6 hamburger buns

Brown ground beef, add remaining ingredients except buns, and heat. Serve on hamburger buns. 6 servings.

Pizza Sandwich

8 thick slices crusty French bread, toasted and buttered
1 can (8 oz.) pizza sauce
8 slices provolone cheese
½ lb. pepperoni sausage, sliced

Spread 2 T pizza sauce on each piece of bread, cover with cheese. Arrange several slices of pepperoni on cheese. Heat 7 minutes in a 450° F. oven or just until the cheese begins to melt. Serve with Italian olives and cherry tomatoes. 8 servings.

Hot Taco Dogs

1 lb. hot dogs
1 can (8 oz.) taco sauce
1 pkg. taco shells (10 to 12)
1 can (7¾ oz.) frozen avocado dip, thawed
Shredded lettuce
Shredded Cheddar cheese

Without cutting all the way through, split hot dogs lengthwise. Simmer in taco sauce 10 minutes. Tuck one hot dog into each taco shell, spoon on thawed avocado dip. Garnish with lettuce, cheese, and a spoonful of taco sauce on each sandwich. 10 servings.

Chihuahuas

10 hot dog buns, toasted
1 pkg. (6 oz.) corn chips
10 hot dogs, grilled
1 can (1 lb.) chili, heated
½ head shredded lettuce
¼ lb. grated Cheddar cheese

Line buns with chips, add hot dogs, top with a large spoonful of chili, shredded lettuce, and cheese. 10 servings.

Tacos

Taco shells are available ready-cooked (deliciously tender crisp), and canned or frozen ready-to-fry. The latter are round flat cakes of corn meal dough called tortillas. When fried in oil and folded tortillas become taco shells.

The shells are filled with a hot chili-seasoned ground meat mixture for which two instants also are available. One is an envelope of seasoning mix which is combined with cooked ground beef and water and simmered a short while. The other is a canned ready-to-eat meat mixture.

Spoon the hot taco meat into taco shells, garnish with finely shredded lettuce and shredded Cheddar or Monterey Jack cheese (plus options like chopped onion, sliced ripe olives, chopped tomato, taco sauce or guacamole) and you've got yourself a taco treat!

Corn Beef Barbeque

1 can (12 oz.) corn beef
½ C barbecue sauce
½ C orange juice
¼ C brown sugar

Combine all ingredients in a saucepan over medium heat. Stir until hot and completely mixed (corn beef will separate). Serve on split hard rolls or hamburger buns. Serves 4.

* * * * *

SALADS

Patio Ham Salad

Follow Patio Salad recipe; page 95. Add 1 C slivered ham and 1 C slivered Swiss cheese just before serving. Serves 6.

Shell Salad with Shrimp

1/3 C olive or salad oil
1/3 C lemon juice
1 envelope Italian salad dressing mix
1 lb. shrimp, cooked and diced
½ lb. pasta shells, cooked
1 pkg. (10 oz.) frozen cut green beans, cooked
1 red onion, cut into thin rings
2 T pimiento, chopped

Combine oil, lemon juice and dressing mix, blending well. Combine remaining ingredients, and dressing mixture. Toss to coat. Refrigerate 1 hour before serving. Serves 4 to 6.

Shrimp-Artichoke Salad

2 lbs. shrimp, medium size, cooked and cleaned
2 pkgs. (10 oz. each) frozen artichoke hearts, cooked
2 cans (8 oz. each) Mandarin oranges
1 head iceberg lettuce, cubed
Vinegar and oil dressing

Combine and chill all ingredients. Just before serving toss with dressing. Serves 8.

Ming Salad

½ C boiled salad dressing
1 8-oz. pkg. cream cheese, softened
1 pkg. (3 oz.) lime gelatin
1 C boiling water
1 can (13 oz.) crushed pineapple plus juice
1½ C diced cooked chicken
½ C celery, sliced
1 t curry powder

Gradually add salad dressing to softened cream cheese.

70

Dissolve gelatin in boiling water, stir in pineapple. Gradually add this mixture to cheese mixture. Fold in chicken, celery and curry powder. Chill until firm in a 1½-qt. mold or 4 to 6 individual molds. Serves 4 to 6.

* * * * *

CHOWDERS

Be sure to serve good bread and plenty of butter with these filling soups. Crusty French, Italian sour dough, dark strong rye breads and, of course, limpa with Swedish Meat Soup.

Tuna Chowder

4 slices bacon
1/3 C frozen minced onions
2 T instant green pepper
1 can (10 oz.) frozen cream of potato soup
2 C milk
1 can (7 oz.) tuna
Paprika

Cook bacon until crisp, drain. In 2 T drippings sauté onion and pepper until tender. Add soup and milk, heat to boiling. Add tuna and bacon, heat through. Sprinkle with paprika when serving. Serves 4.

Mother Wyler's Seafood Gumbo

1 can (7½ oz.) crabmeat
1 can (10½ oz.) pepper pot soup
1 can (10½ oz.) chicken gumbo soup
1 can (14½ oz.) evaporated milk

Combine all ingredients and simmer 5 minutes. Serves 5 or 6.

Green Bean Soup

1 can (1 lb.) tomatoes
1 can (1 lb.) cut green beans plus juice
1 can (10¾ oz.) Cheddar cheese soup
1 T butter
½ t salt
¼ t basil

Combine all ingredients and simmer 10 minutes. Serves 4 to 6.

Oyster Chowder

1 can (10 oz.) frozen cream of potato soup, thawed
1 C milk
1 can (10½ oz.) oyster stew
1 can (8 oz.) oysters, including liquid
1 can (8 oz.) green peas, including liquid
1 can (8 oz.) whole kernel corn, including liquid
1 T butter
1 T instant minced onion
1 t Worcestershire sauce
Few drops Tabasco sauce

Combine all ingredients and simmer 5 minutes. Serves 6.

Fisherman's Favorite Chowder

¼ lb. bacon, diced
6 C water
1 can (14½ oz.) evaporated milk
1 envelope onion soup mix
2 lbs. boneless fish fillets, cut in 1-inch pieces
1 envelope (4-serving size) instant mashed potatoes

Sauté bacon until crisp. Add water, milk and onion soup mix, heat to boiling. Add fish, simmer 10 minutes or until fish is done. Stir in instant potato mix. Heat through. Serves 12.

Clam Chowder

1 envelope potato leek soup mix
1 can (7½ oz.) minced clams, plus juice
1 T butter
1 T frozen chopped chives

Prepare soup mix as directed, but reduce water by ½ C. Add remaining ingredients, heat and serve. Serves 3.

Swedish Meat Soup

½ lb. ground beef
⅛ t nutmeg
½ t salt
1 T butter
1 pkg. (10 oz.) cut cabbage frozen in butter sauce, thawed
1 envelope onion soup mix, prepared as directed

Combine ground beef, nutmeg and salt. Shape in small balls and brown in butter. Add meatballs and cabbage to prepared onion soup. Heat through. Serves 4.

Corn Chowder

1 envelope creamy onion sauce mix
2 C milk
1 can (1 lb.) cream-style corn
Herb-seasoned croutons

Combine sauce mix, milk and corn. Heat, stirring constantly. Do not boil. Serve garnished with croutons. Serves 4.

Chapter 4

Breakfast and Brunch

Eggs
Let's Cook It In The Oven
Etc. . . .
Sweet Toppings For Pancakes and Waffles

To my way of thinking, the ideal breakfast is one my family gets for themselves. But if you like to cook breakfast, have to cook breakfast, or if you entertain at breakfasts or brunches, you'll find here a variety of excellent time-saving recipes.

*   *   *   *   *

EGGS

Breakfast on the Run

1 C milk
1 egg
½ C favorite fruit, fresh or canned (bananas, apricots, strawberries) etc.

Place ingredients in a blender container and blend on low speed until well mixed. One serving.

Mushroom Scrambled Eggs

6 eggs
¾ C milk
1 envelope mushroom soup mix or beef-flavor mushroom mix
Butter

Beat together eggs, milk and soup mix. Cook over medium heat using about 2 T butter. Serves 3.

Golden Eggs

1 can (10¾ oz.) condensed cheese soup
1 T milk
2 T sauterne
6 eggs

Combine soup, milk and wine. Pour half the mixture into greased baking dish, 10 x 6-inches. Carefully break eggs into sauce. Pour remaining cheese sauce over eggs. Bake uncovered 20 minutes at 325° F. Serve on toast. Serves 3.

Eggs in Tomato Sauce

1 jar (16 oz.) tomato or marinara sauce
Pinch Italian seasoning
6 eggs
Salt and pepper to taste

Mix tomato sauce and Italian seasoning in an 8- or 10-inch skillet. Heat to simmer. Beat eggs, add salt and pepper to taste. Pour egg mixture into simmering sauce, cover and cook just until set. Serves 3.

Cheese Omelet

6 eggs
1/3 C milk
1 envelope cheese sauce mix
2 T butter

Beat together eggs, milk and cheese sauce mix. Melt butter in skillet, add egg mixture and cook slowly. When eggs are set but still moist fold omelet over and serve. Serves 3.

Eggs Stroganoff

4 eggs, poached
4 English muffin halves, toasted
1 envelope Stroganoff or sour cream sauce mix, prepared as
    directed

Place poached eggs on toasted muffin halves. Pour prepared sauce over all and serve. Serves 2.

* * * * *

LET'S COOK IT IN THE OVEN

Baked Mushroom Omelet

½ lb. mushrooms, sliced
¼ C butter
8 eggs, beaten
1 t salt
¼ t pepper
¼ t rosemary

Sauté mushrooms in butter. Combine with remaining ingre-
dients and turn into a buttered baking pan, 7 x 11-inches.
Bake at 325° F. for 15 minutes or just until eggs are set.
Serves 4.

Oven-Cooked Bacon

Arrange slices of bacon in a shallow baking pan (a jelly
roll pan is ideal). Bake 20 minutes at 350° F. Don't turn
the bacon. It will cook evenly on both sides and remain
flat. When serving bacon with Oven French Toast cook
the bacon in a separate pan at the same temperature (500°
F.) for the same length of time (14 minutes), but check
after 10 minutes.

Oven-Baked Sausage Pancakes

Pancake mix for 8 pancakes, prepared as directed
1 pkg. (8 oz.) brown and serve sausages

Pour prepared pancake batter into well greased 9 x 13-inch baking pan. Arrange sausages in batter. Bake at 450° F. for 12 to 15 minutes. Cut in squares to serve. (For larger amounts, double the pancake batter, use a 12 x 17-inch pan; bake at the same temperature, same length of time.) Do not expect these pancakes to brown on top; they look more like cake than pancakes. Serves 3 to 4.

Oven French Toast

2 eggs
½ C milk
¼ t salt
Dash nutmeg
8 slices French or Italian bread
¼ C butter, melted

Beat together lightly the eggs, milk, salt and nutmeg. Dip both sides of each piece of bread in egg mixture. Place in a greased, shallow baking pan and drizzle melted butter over bread. Bake at 500° F. for 7 minutes per side or until brown. Serves 4.

* * * * *

ETC....

Blueberry Pancakes

1 pkg. (14 oz.) blueberry muffin mix
1 egg
1 C milk
½ t grated orange rind

Rinse blueberries and drain. Combine muffin mix, egg, milk and orange rind. Beat until well blended. Fold in blueberries. Fry on a greased griddle until the tops bubble. Turn and brown the other side. Makes 20 fine-textured 4-inch pancakes. Serve with orange marmalade, blueberry syrup or your favorite topping. Serves 6.

Potato Nest Eggs

2 C mashed potatoes (prepare 4 servings instant potatoes)
1 egg
¼ C grated cheese
1 t onion juice
4 eggs (additional)
Salt and papper to taste

Blend mashed potatoes, egg, cheese and onion juice. Shape in 4 balls and place on a greased baking sheet. Indent center of each ball; break egg into each potato nest. Season with salt and pepper. Bake at 325° F. for 20 minutes or until eggs are firm. Serves 4.

Country Breakfast

6 slices bacon
1 pkg. (1½ lbs.) frozen potatoes O'Brien
1 t salt
¼ t pepper
6 eggs
1 pkg. (4 oz.) grated sharp Cheddar cheese (optional)

78

Cook bacon until crisp; remove from skillet. Pour off all but 2 T bacon fat. Add potatoes, season with salt and pepper and cook according to directions on potato package. Carefully break 6 eggs over potato mixture, cover and cook until egg whites are firm. Garnish with bacon strips, sprinkle with grated cheese. Cover and heat a moment longer until cheese just begins to melt. Serves 4 to 6.

Breakfast Casserole

2 T butter
1 pkg. (8 oz.) brown and serve sausages
1 can (20 oz.) sliced apples
1/3 C sugar
Dash salt
Dash nutmeg

In an attractive, table-going skillet melt butter, brown the sausages, add apples, sugar, salt and nutmeg. Heat until sugar is melted and apples are slightly brown. Serve with buttered toast, sweet rolls or scrambled eggs, etc. Serves 3 to 4.

Rumaki Brunch

1½ lbs. chicken livers (24 livers)
½ lb. sliced bacon (12 slices), cut in half
2 cans (16 oz. each) pineapple chunks, drained
16 frozen waffles

Wrap livers with bacon slices and secure with toothpicks. Bake in a large, shallow baking pan, 10 minutes at 350° F. Drain off fat, add pineapple and continue baking for another 10 minutes. Place waffles in oven to heat during these last 10 minutes. Serve with honey. Serves 8.

* * * * *

SWEET TOPPINGS FOR PANCAKES
AND WAFFLES

Hot Sausage Syrup

½ lb. pork sausage meat
1½ C pancake syrup

Shape pork sausage in small balls (1-inch diameter). Fry until thoroughly cooked. Drain fat and add syrup; heat to boiling. Serve hot. Makes 2½ cups.

Blueberry Syrup

1 can (21 oz.) blueberry pie filling
½ C water
½ t lemon rind

Combine ingredients and heat through. Serve hot. Makes 3 cups.

Honey and Almond Butter

½ C butter, softened
½ C honey
¼ C chopped toasted almonds

Beat honey into softened butter. Stir in nuts. Makes 1¼ cups.

Mixed Fruit Glacé

2 pkgs. (10 oz.) frozen mixed fruit, plus juice
1 jar (8 oz.) crabapple jelly

Thaw fruit according to package directions. (This takes less than 10 minutes.) Melt jelly over low heat. Combine fruit, including the juice, and melted jelly. To serve: spoon over pancakes, waffles, ice cream or sherbet. Makes 3 cups.

For additional sauce and topping recipes, see:
Basic Sweet Sauce, p. 163
Cider Sauce, p. 162
Pineapple Sauce, p. 163
Apricot Sauce, p. 163
Cinnamon Sauce, p. 163
Sour Cream Topping, p. 162

For additional breakfast and brunch recipes see:
Danish Soufflé, p. 65
Cheese Soufflé, p. 66

Chapter 5

Vegetables

Vegetables are best unadorned, I believe. Cook the freshest or the finest frozen variety you can find to a crunchy-tender state, add a bit of seasoning and a nub of butter, and that's the way vegetables *ought* to taste! One hardly needs a recipe for such a rule. On the other hand, there is the desire for variety in our meals plus an occasional need for camouflage. Therefore, this chapter on vegetables.

Mushrooms Parmesan

Don't be overzealous when cleaning fresh mushrooms; just rinse them. The experts tell us when mushrooms are peeled or scrubbed some of the best flavor is lost.

1½ lbs. whole fresh mushrooms
¼ C olive or vegetable oil
¾ C Italian-style bread crumbs
2 T parsley flakes
¼ C Parmesan cheese
1 t garlic salt

Toss mushrooms with half the oil in a 1½-qt. casserole. Combine the dry ingredients and sprinkle over mushrooms. Pour the remaining oil over all. Bake 25 minutes at 350° F. Serves 4 to 6.

Barbecued Onions

Thread small canned onions on skewers. Brush with French dressing and broil until brown.

Favorite Green Bean Casserole

Wonderfully flavored and glamorous enough for company.

2 pkgs. (10 oz. each) frozen French-style green beans, prepared as directed
1 can (10½ oz.) cream of celery, mushroom, or chicken soup
1 can (3½ oz.) French fried onions

Combine cooked green beans, soup, and onions, reserving a few onions for garnish, in a 1½-qt. casserole. Bake 30 minutes at 350° F. Serves 6.

Italian Green Beans

1 pkg. (10 oz.) frozen Italian green beans
2 T butter or Italian-seasoned salad dressing
1 jar (2 oz.) sliced mushrooms
1 T pimiento, diced

Cook and season beans as directed on pkg. Drain. Add butter, mushrooms and pimiento. Stir gently over medium heat until all ingredients are heated through. Serves 3.

Cauliflower and Green Beans with Cheese Sauce

1 can (10½ oz.) Cheddar cheese soup
½ C milk
Dash cayenne pepper
1 pkg. (10 oz.) frozen green beans, cooked and seasoned as directed
1 pkg. (10 oz.) frozen cauliflower, cooked and seasoned as directed

Gradually stir milk into cheese soup. Season with cayenne and continue to stir while heating to a boil. Combine cooked vegetables in a serving dish and pour cheese sauce over all. Serves 6.

Scalloped Tomatoes

1 can (1 lb. 13 oz.) tomatoes
2 T oil
½ t salt
¼ t pepper
⅛ t basil
1 can (3 oz.) chow mein noodles, coarsely crushed
Parmesan cheese

Blend tomatoes, oil and seasonings. In a greased 1½-qt.
baking dish alternate layers of tomato mixture and noodles,
ending with noodles. Sprinkle with Parmesan cheese. Bake
20 minutes at 375° F. Serves 4 to 6.

Lima Bean Casserole

1 pkg. (10 oz.) frozen lima beans
2 T instant minced onions
⅛ t pepper
1 can (10½) cream of chicken soup

Place frozen beans in a small casserole. Sprinkle with onion
and pepper. Cover with soup. Bake covered for 1 hour at
350° F. Serves 3.

Baked Beans

1 can (3½ oz.) French fried onions
1 can deviled ham (4½ oz.)
1 T molasses
1 t prepared mustard
¼ t salt
2 cans (1 lb. each) pork and beans, Boston style
1 can (8 oz.) tomato sauce

Combine half the onions and all other ingredients. Bake in
a beanpot or 1½-qt. casserole 30 minutes at 350° F.
Sprinkle remaining onions on top during last 5 minutes.
Serves 6 to 8.

Party Vegetable Casserole

1 can (1 lb.) diagonally cut wax beans
1 can (1 lb.) small onions
1 can (10½ oz.) cream of mushroom soup
2 T pimiento, diced
¼ C packaged bread crumbs
¼ C grated Parmesan cheese
2 T butter, melted

In a 1½-qt. casserole combine beans, onions, soup and pimiento. Sprinkle mixture of crumbs, cheese and butter over top. Bake 30 minutes at 325° F. Serves 6 to 8.

Creamed Onions

1 can (16 oz.) small whole onions, plus liquid
1 envelope white sauce mix
Paprika

Use liquid from onions as part of liquid requirement in sauce mix. Proceed with sauce mix preparation as directed. Add onions and simmer gently until heated through. Transfer to a serving dish; sprinkle with paprika. Serves 3 or 4.

Asparagus Romanoff

1 can (10½ oz.) Cheddar cheese soup
2 t Worcestershire sauce
½ C sour cream
2 lbs. fresh asparagus, cooked, or 2 cans (19 oz. each) asparagus spears, heated

In a saucepan over low heat combine soup, Worcestershire sauce, and sour cream. Stir constantly and heat to just below boiling. Arrange hot cooked asparagus on serving platter. Pour sauce over asparagus and serve. If desired, run the asparagus and sauce under the broiler for a minute or two before serving. Serves 8.

Corn Pudding

Topped with maple syrup and a dollop of whipped cream, this slightly sweet corn pudding could also be served for dessert.

1 pkg. real egg custard
1 C milk
1 can (16 oz.) cream-style corn
1 T butter, cut in dots

Stir custard mix into milk, add butter and corn. Bake in a 1-qt. casserole for 1 hour in a 350° F. oven. Serves 4.

Baked Eggplant

1 medium eggplant
¼ C milk
½ C Italian-seasoned crumbs
¼ C butter

Pare eggplant, ¾ inch thick. Dip each slice in milk and coat with crumbs. Melt butter in a shallow baking pan. Place slices in butter, then turn so as to coat both sides. Bake 20 minutes at 400° F. Serves 6.

Cabbage Casserole

2 pkgs. (10 oz. each) cabbage frozen in butter sauce, cooked as directed
1 can (10½ oz.) cream of celery soup
8 strips bacon, fried crisp and diced
¼ C packaged bread crumbs
1 T butter, melted

In a 1½-qt. casserole blend hot cooked cabbage and butter sauce, soup and bacon. Combine crumbs and butter and sprinkle over top. Bake 15 minutes at 400° F. Serves 4 to 6.

Broccoli and Sour Cream Sauce

1 can (10½ oz.) cream of celery soup
½ C sour cream
2 pkgs. (10 oz. each) frozen broccoli, cooked and seasoned
    as directed

Blend and heat soup and sour cream just short of boiling
point. Pour over cooked broccoli. Serves 6.

Baked Sweet Potatoes

¼ C butter
2 cans (1 lb. each) sweet potatoes
¼ C pancake syrup
½ C pre-sweetened cereal, crushed

Melt butter in baking dish. Roll sweet potatoes in butter,
dribble syrup over potatoes and sprinkle with cereal. Bake
30 minutes at 350° F. Serves 4 to 6.

Brussels Sprouts in Garlic Sauce

1 pkg. (10 oz.) Brussels sprouts frozen in butter sauce,
    cooked as directed
1½ t lemon juice
⅛ t garlic salt
Pepper to taste

Empty cooking pouch into serving dish. Stir in garlic salt
and lemon juice; sprinkle with pepper. Serves 2 to 3.

Barbecued Corn

2 can (12 oz. each) white corn, plus liquid
1 8-oz. jar stuffed olives, sliced
1 C barbecue sauce

Combine all ingredients and simmer 5 minutes. Serves 6.

Minted Peas

1 pkg. (10 oz.) frozen peas, cooked as directed and drained
2 T butter
2 T apple mint jelly
⅛ t mace

Add butter, jelly and mace to hot drained peas. Stir gently over low heat until jelly and butter are melted. Serves 3.

Green Goddess Peas

1 pkg. (10 oz.) frozen peas, cooked as directed
2 to 4 T green goddess salad dressing

Stir salad dressing into hot peas. Stir gently over low heat until heated through. This basic idea goes a long way. Try any likely salad dressing with other hot cooked vegetables. The combination possibilities are fascinating. Serves 3.

Zucchini and Mushrooms

1 pkg. (10 oz.) frozen mushrooms in butter sauce
4 medium zucchini, sliced ¼ inch thick
½ t salt

Remove frozen mushrooms from pouch and place in a saucepan. Add salt and zucchini. Cover and cook over medium heat 10 to 15 minutes or until zucchini is barely tender. Serves 4.

Chili Beans

2 cans (21 oz.) pork and beans
1 envelope chili mix
1 T molasses

Combine all ingredients in a saucepan and simmer until hot. Or, bake 45 minutes at 350° F. Serves 6 to 8.

Caraway and Cabbage

1 pkg. (10 oz.) frozen cabbage in butter sauce, cooked as
   directed
¼ C sour cream
½ t caraway seed

Empty cooking pouch of cabbage into serving dish. Blend
in sour cream and caraway, tossing gently to mix. Serves 2
to 3.

Arlaine's Spinach-Filled Tomatoes

6 medium to large tomatoes
1 pkg. (12 oz.) frozen spinach soufflé, barely thawed

Hollow out tomatoes and drain. Spoon thawed spinach
soufflé into tomato shells, being careful not to overfill.
Place each tomato in a foil baking cup on a baking sheet.
Bake 25 minutes at 350° F. Serves 6.

Creamed Spinach

2 pkgs. (10 oz. each) frozen chopped spinach, cooked
1 can (10½ oz.) cream of celery soup
Dash nutmeg

Drain cooked spinach. Stir in soup and nutmeg. Heat and
serve. Serves 6.

Baked Onions

Wrap peeled sweet onions (medium to large) securely
in foil and roast over hot coals 45 to 60 minutes. Turn
occasionally.

For additional vegetable recipes, see:
Side Dishes, Chapter 6, page 90, for white potato recipes.
Broccoli and Macaroni, Italian style, p. 98
Noodles with Spinach Sauce, p. 96

Chapter 6

Side Dishes

Potatoes
Rice
Noodles
Macaroni
Others

A side dish is defined in Webster's as "one of the foods subordinate to the main course." In this chapter the side dishes are limited to potatoes and the kinds of food we often substitute for potatoes.

* * * * *

POTATOES

Potatoes Vesuvius

6 C prepared hot mashed potatoes (follow directions for 12
    servings of instant potatoes)
¼ C butter
2 eggs
1 can (10½ oz.) Cheddar cheese soup
⅛ t pepper
¼ t dry mustard

Beat butter and eggs into prepared hot mashed potatoes. (The butter is *in addition to* what has been used in the preparation of the potatoes.) Spoon potato mixture into a 2-quart casserole, leaving a depression in the center. Stir pepper and mustard into cheese soup and pour into center of potatoes. Bake 20 to 25 minutes at 375° F. Serves 8 to 10.

Buttered New Potatoes

A speedy cook never peels potatoes if she can avoid it!

2 cans (1 lb.) small whole potatoes
Salt and pepper to taste
¼ C butter
1 T parsley flakes

Drain potatoes, rinse and pat dry. Sprinkle with salt and pepper to taste. Melt butter in a skillet, add potatoes. Heat slowly, occasionally tossing potatoes in butter to coat. Sprinkle with parsley just before serving. Serves 4 to 6.
  Suggestion: Place drained, whole potatoes in roasting pan alongside a roast 20 minutes before roast is finished. Baste once or twice with pan juices.

California Baked Potatoes

4 to 6 baked potatoes
1 C California Dip, p. 174

Split baked potatoes and top with a dollop of dip before serving.

Potatoes Au Gratin

1 pkg. (12 oz.) frozen hash brown potatoes
1 C milk
2 T butter
½ t seasoned pepper
1 t seasoned salt
¼ C sliced green onion or frozen chopped onion
1½ C grated Cheddar cheese (6 oz.)

Spread potatoes in a shallow casserole. Scald milk with butter and seasonings. Sprinkle onions and cheese over potatoes and pour milk mixture over all. Cover and bake 30 minutes at 350° F. Serves 3 to 4.

German Potato Salad

4 slices bacon
2 cans (1 lb. each) sliced potatoes
2 T frozen chives
½ C creamy onion salad dressing
½ t salt
⅛ t pepper

Fry bacon until crisp, and drain on paper towel. Pour off all but 1 T of fat from skillet. Add potatoes, which have been rinsed and patted dry on paper towels. Toss in remaining ingredients and heat through. Crumble bacon and sprinkle over potatoes. Serve immediately. Serves 4 to 6.

Potatoes A La King

1 can (1 lb.) sliced potatoes
1 envelope white sauce mix (or a la king sauce mix, prepared as directed
1 t Worcestershire sauce
Paprika

Drain potatoes, rinse and pat dry. Combine them with the prepared sauce mix and Worcestershire sauce. Heat. Sprinkle with paprika before serving. Serves 3.

Mashed Potatoes and Chives

If you are not yet satisfied with the flavor of instant mashed potatoes try another brand. If that doesn't work try chives.

4 servings instant mashed potatoes, prepared as directed
1 T frozen chopped chives

Add chives to boiling water just before adding other ingredients. Serves 4.

Cheese Scalloped Potatoes

1 can (10½ oz.) condensed Cheddar cheese soup
Dash cayenne pepper
½ C milk
½ C sliced stuffed olives or ¼ C frozen chopped onion
2 cans (1 lb. each) sliced potaotes

Combine soup, pepper and milk. Pour over layers of potato and olives in a 1½-qt. casserole. Bake at 350° F. for
25 minutes. Serves 6.

Potato Puff Casserole

8 servings instant mashed potatoes, prepared as directed
        (4 C hot mashed potatoes)
1 pkg. (8 oz.) cream cheese, softened
1 egg beaten
1/3 C frozen minced onion
1 jar (2 oz.) pimiento, chopped
1 t salt
Pepper

Blend softened cream cheese into hot potatoes. Stir in remaining ingredients. Bake in a 1-quart casserole at 350° F.
for 45 minutes. Serves 6.

Scalloped Potatoes

1 pkg. scalloped potato mix, prepared as directed
½ t carroway seed
1 T frozen chopped chives or frozen minced onion

Add carroway seed and chives to potato mixture just before baking. Serves 3 to 4.

93

Peanut Potato Salad

1 pint prepared potato salad
½ C salted peanuts

Combine ingredients just before serving. Serves 3.

* * * * *

RICE

Virginia's Baked Rice

1½ C instant rice
2 T butter
1½ C water
1 t salt
1 envelope French dressing mix
1 2-oz. can sliced mushrooms, plus liquid
1 tomato, sliced thin
1 t frozen chives

In a 1½-quart flameproof casserole, lightly brown rice in butter. Add 1½ C hot water, salt, dressing mix, and mushrooms and their liquid. Cover casserole and bake 20 minutes at 350° F. During last 10 minutes of baking top with thinly sliced tomato and sprinkle with chives. Serves 4 to 6.

Nice Rice Combination

1½ C instant rice, prepared as directed
2 cans (12 oz.) Mexicorn, drained
1 t salt
1 t instant minced onion
¼ t pepper
2 T chopped pimiento

In a 2-quart saucepan, prepare instant rice as directed on package. After steaming process is complete, stir in remaining ingredients. Heat and serve. Serves 6 to 8.

Spanish Rice

Spanish Rice is available canned, frozen, as a seasoning mix, a seasoning and rice mix, and a seasoning, rice and macaroni mix. Here's another fast way to make it.

4 slices bacon, diced
¼ C diced green pepper
1 1/3 C instant rice (1 small box)
1 envelope onion soup mix
1 can (No. 2½) tomatoes

Fry bacon until almost crisp, add pepper and rice and sauté a few minutes more. Stir in remaining ingredients and bring to a boil. Simmer covered 5 minutes. Serves 4 to 6.

Boo's Rice Patio Salad

Looking for something to take the place of potato salad? This is it!

1 pkg. (10 oz.) frozen peas
½ t salt
1½ C water
1 1/3 C instant rice
1 T frozen minced onion
¾ C mayonnaise
½ C dill pickle, chopped

In a covered saucepan bring peas, salt and water to a boil. Remove from heat and stir in instant rice and onion. Cover and let stand for 13 minutes. Cool. Stir in mayonnaise and pickle. Chill. Serves 6.

Sour Cream Pilaff

1 pkg. (8 oz.) chicken-flavored rice-macaroni mix
1 bay leaf
1 can (2 oz.) sliced mushrooms
1 C sour cream
2 T frozen chopped chives

Prepare rice-macaroni mix as directed, but add bay leaf to chicken broth. When rice mixture is cooked remove bay leaf and stir in mushrooms and sour cream. Garnish with chives and serve immediately. Serves 4 to 6.

* * * * *

NOODLES

Fettucine

1 lb. egg noodles
1 stick butter (½ C)
1 C half-and-half cream
1 C grated Parmesan cheese

Cook noodles according to package directions. Drain. Heat cream and butter over low heat until butter melts. Pour over noodles and sprinkle with cheese. Toss until noodles are evenly coated. Serves 8.

Noodles With Spinach Sauce

1 pkg. noodles Romanoff mix, prepared as directed
1 pkg. (12 oz.) chopped spinach, prepared as directed

Stir hot cooked spinach, well drained, into hot noodles and sauce mixture until well blended. Serves 4.

1 pkg. (6 oz.) noodles almondine mix
1 T frozen chives
½ t salt
2 eggs, separated

Follow saucepan method and measurements on noodle package. Add chives, salt and egg yolks to noodles and sauce mixture before bringing to a boil. Heat mixture to bubbling only; it will be thick. Meanwhile, toast almonds in noodle package to a golden brown in the oven. Beat egg whites to soft peaks and quickly fold into noodle mixture, along with half of the almonds. Turn into a 1½-quart casserole. Sprinkle with remaining almonds. Bake 20 minutes at 350° F. Serves 4 to 6.

* * * * *

MACARONI

Macaroni Salad

1 C mayonnaise
¼ C vinegar
¼ C milk
1 envelope onion salad dressing mix
6 C cooked macaroni (shell, elbow, etc.)
2 hard-cooked eggs, chopped
½ C celery, diced
1 T pimiento, chopped (optional)
2 T anchovies, cut up (optional)

Blend mayonnaise, vinegar, milk and salad dressing mix. Place remaining ingredients in a bowl, add dressing and toss until well mixed. Serve at once or chill. Serves 8.

Macaroni Casserole

1 pkg. macaroni and cheese dinner, prepared as directed
1 C tomatoes
½ C sour cream
6 slices bacon, cooked crisp and crumbled
½ t salt
Pepper to taste

Combine ingredients and mix well. Place in baking dish and bake 30 minutes at 350° F. Serves 4 to 6.

Broccoli and Macaroni, Italian Style

1 pkg. frozen chopped broccoli, cooked as directed
1 garlic clove
1 pkg. macaroni and cheese mix, prepared as directed
¼ C Parmesan cheese

Add garlic clove to broccoli as it cooks; discard when broccoli is done. Combine prepared macaroni and cheese with drained broccoli. Sprinkle with Parmesan cheese before serving. Serves 4 to 6.

* * * * *

OTHERS

Stuffing Casserole

1 can (10½ oz.) onion soup
¼ C butter
½ t poultry seasoning
4 C seasoned stuffing mix
½ C diced celery

Heat soup as it comes from the can. Add butter and stir until melted. Add seasoning. Stir in stuffing mix and celery. Bake in greased 1- or 1½-quart covered casserole 30-minutes at 350° F. Serves 4 to 6.

Dumplings With Sour Cream Sauce

6 to 8 frozen dumplings
1 can (10½ oz.) cream of chicken soup
1 C sour cream

Cook dumplings as directed on package. Combine soup and sour cream. Heat to just below boiling. Arrange dumplings on a serving platter and ladle sauce over dumplings. Or, serve sauce and dumplings separately. Serves 6 to 8.

Yorkshire Pudding

Although properly called a bread, Yorkshire pudding is eaten as that filling portion of a meal designated in this chapter. It is traditionally served with a roast of beef.

1 pkg. (6 oz.) popover mix, prepared as directed
½ C beef drippings

Heat beef drippings in a 9 x 13-inch baking pan. The pan should be very hot. Pour prepared popover mix over the drippings and bake at 400° F. for 30 minutes. To serve, cut in squares and serve immediately with roast beef and gravy. Serves 6.

For additional side dish recipes, see:
Chili and Rice, p. 59

Chapter 7

Salads and Dressings

Fruit Salads
Dressings for Fruit Salads
Vegetable Salads
Dressings for Vegetable Salads
Packaged and Canned Additions to a Tossed Salad

See Side Dishes, Chapter 6, page 90, for potato, rice and macaroni salads.

See Luncheon and Supper Entrees, Chapter 3, page 61, for chicken, seafood and meat salads.

* * * * *

FRUIT SALADS

Frozen Fruit Salad

1 envelope whipped topping mix
¼ t almond extract
1 pkg. (3 oz.) cream cheese, softened
1 can (1 lb.) apricot halves
1 can (1 lb.) pineapple chunks or tidbits
1 jar (4 oz.) maraschino cherries
1 C miniature marshmallows

Prepare whipped topping mix according to package directions, adding almond extract. Beat in softened cream cheese. Fold in drained fruits and marshmallows. Freeze in 9 x 9-inch pan several hours or overnight. Individual servings may be frozen in paper baking cups. Serves 9 to 12.

Melon Balls in Wine

2 pkgs. (10 oz. each) frozen mixed melon balls or 4 C fresh
    melon balls
2 t sugar
1 C dry white wine

Thaw melon balls to room temperature, and drain. Sprinkle
with sugar, add wine. Chill, turning melon balls occasionally in the wine. Serve in compotes or on a bed of lettuce.
Serves 4.

Cranberry-Orange Relish Mold

1 jar (14 oz.) cranberry-orange relish
¼ C chopped pecans or walnuts
1 pkg. (3 oz.) cherry or raspberry gelatin, prepared as di-
    rected

Stir cranberry-orange relish and nuts into slightly thickened
gelatin mixture. Pour into a 1-qt. mold and chill firm.
Serves 6.

Quick-Jell Raspberry Salad

1 pkg. (3 oz.) raspberry gelatin
1 C boiling water
1 pkg. (10 oz.) frozen raspberries

Dissolve gelatin in boiling water. Stir in frozen fruit until
it thaws. Pour into 3-cup mold and chill until firm. Serves
3 to 4.

Quick-Jell Strawberry Salad

Follow recipe above, but substitute strawberry gelatin
and frozen strawberries for the raspberry ingredients.

5 Cup Salad

This recipe has been around for over twenty years that I'm aware of, and it's still being discovered and appreciated. I've heard it called Hawaiian Salad, Half-Cup Salad, 1-2-3-4 Salad, 5 Cup Salad, and Overnite Salad. The last title is a misnomer; the salad is best eaten the day it's made.

1 C crushed pineapple
1 C mandarin oranges
1 C coconut
1 C miniature marshmallows
1 C sour cream

Drain fruit, combine all ingredients, and chill. Serves 6.

Strawberry Dessert Salad

Follow recipe for 5 Cup Salad but omit crushed pineapple and oranges. Substitute 1 can (13 oz.) frozen pineapple chunks, partially thawed and drained, and 1 C whole fresh strawberries. Serves 6.

Orange Sherbet Salad

1 pkg. (6 oz.) orange gelatin
2 C boiling water
1 pint orange sherbet
1 can (11 oz.) mandarin oranges

Dissolve gelatin in boiling water. Stir in sherbet until melted; add oranges. Pour into 1½-qt. ring mold and chill until firm. Serves 6.

Honeydew Melon Salad

Pare and seed a honeydew melon. Cut in ½-inch slices. Place a serving of Cherry Cola Salad in the center of each slice and top with a dollop of Honey Almond dressing, page 104. Serves 6 to 8.

Lynn's Frosted Party Salad

1 pkg. (6 oz.) orange gelatin
2 C boiling water
1 can (12 oz.) frozen orange juice concentrate
1 can (8 oz.) mandarin oranges, drained
1 can (12 oz.) crushed pineapple, drained

Dissolve gelatin in boiling water. Stir in frozen concentrate.
Add fruit and pour into a 9 x 13-inch pan. Chill until firm.
Top with the following "frosting".

1 pkg. (3 oz.) instant lemon pudding
1 C cold milk
1 envelope whipped topping mix, prepared as directed

Blend pudding mix with cold milk following pkg. directions. Fold prepared topping into pudding mixture. Spread
on gelatin layer, chill. Serves 10 to 12.

Cherry Cola Salad

1 bottle (10 oz.) regular or diet cola, heated
1 pkg. (3 oz.) cherry gelatin
1 can (17 oz.) dark sweet pitted cherries, plus juice

Dissolve gelatin in hot cola; stir in cherries and juice. Chill
until set. Serves 4.

* * * * *

DRESSINGS FOR FRUIT SALADS

Lime Wine Dressing

1 can (6 oz.) frozen limeade concentrate, thawed
¼ C sherry

Stir ingredients together and pour over tossed fruit salad.
Terrific! Makes 1 cup.

Lemon Wine Dressing

Use recipe on previous page but substitute lemonade concentrate for the limeade concentrate.

Orange Cream Dressing

1 T orange juice or 1 t grated orange rind
¼ C maple syrup or honey
1 pkg. (3 oz.) cream cheese, softened

Beat orange juice and syrup into softened cream cheese. Makes about ¾ cup.

Honey Almond Dressing

¼ C honey
¼ t almond extract
1 pkg. (3 oz.) cream cheese, softened
¼ C chopped almonds, optional

Beat honey and extract into softened cream cheese until smooth and fluffy. Fold in nuts. Makes 1 cup.

Vineyard Dressing

2 pkgs. (3 oz. each) cream cheese, softened
½ C mayonnaise
2/3 C white wine

Combine softened cream cheese and mayonnaise. Gradually beat in wine. Make 2 cups.

Honey-Mustard Dressing

1 envelope whipped topping mix
2 T prepared mustard
2 T honey

Prepare whipped topping mix as directed, but add honey and mustard while beating. Makes 2 cups.

* * * * *

VEGETABLE SALADS

Karen's Tomato Aspic

1 pkg. (3 oz.) lemon gelatin
1 C boiling water
Dash cloves
1 t vinegar
1 t onion juice
1 T Worcestershire sauce
1 can (13 oz.) tomato puree or 1 can (16 oz.) tomato sauce

Dissolve gelatin in boiling water. Stir in remaining ingredients. Pour into a mold and chill until firm. Serves 4 to 6.

Tomato Cups

1 can (12 oz.) Mexicorn, drained
½ C oil and vinegar dressing
2 t frozen minced onion
6 whole tomatoes (fresh or canned)

Pour dressing over corn and add onions. Scoop out pulp from center of tomatoes and fill with corn mixture. Serve cold on lettuce leaves. Serves 6.

Cole Slaw

6 C shredded cabbage
½ C salted peanuts
1 can (10 oz.) mandarin oranges, drained and chilled
1 C Italian salad dressing

Combine all ingredients; toss thoroughly. Serves 8.

French Bean Salad

3 pkgs. (10 oz. each) frozen French-style green beans
1 bottle (8 oz.) onion salad dressing
1 t salt
1 large red onion

Cook beans only until tender crisp; drain and cool. Add dressing and salt, toss lightly and marinate in refrigerator 3 hours. To serve, drain beans, arrange servings on lettuce leaf and top with slices of onion. Serves 8.

California Cole Slaw

1 pkg. cole slaw mix or 4 to 6 C shredded cabbage, carrots
    and green pepper
½ pint sour cream
½ envelope onion soup mix
2 t wine vinegar

Blend sour cream and soup mix; add cabbage mixture and vinegar. Toss until well blended. Chill. Serves 4 to 6.

Mexican Avocado Salad

2 cans (7¾ oz. each) frozen avocado dip, thawed
1 can (4 oz.) taco sauce
Garlic salt to taste (optional)

Stir taco sauce into avocado dip. Serve cold on individual lettuce leaves and sprinkle lightly with garlic salt if desired. Serves 6.

Classic Three Bean Salad

1 can (1 lb.) kidney beans
1 can (1 lb.) yellow wax beans
1 can (1 lb.) cut green beans
½ C frozen minced onions
1 bottle (8 oz.) oil and vinegar dressing

Combine all ingredients and marinate overnight in the refrigerator. Serves 8.

Three Bean Salad, Western Style

Follow recipe for Classic Three Bean Salad, but substitute 1 can (1 lb.) garbanzo beans (chick peas) for the yellow wax beans.

* * * * *

DRESSINGS FOR VEGETABLE SALADS

Creamy Garlic Dressing

1 C mayonnaise
1 C buttermilk
1 envelope garlic salad dressing mix

Combine ingredients and blend well. This dressing keeps nicely in the refrigerator for two weeks. Makes 2 cups.

Avocado Dressing

2 avocados, mashed
¾ C herb and garlic French dressing

Combine and beat well. Makes about 2 cups.

Chef's Dressing

1 envelope old-fashioned French salad dressing mix
Tarragon vinegar
1 can (2¼ oz.) chopped black olives

Prepare salad dressing mix (using tarragon vinegar) as directed. Add chopped olives. Makes about 1 1/3 cups.

Sour Cream and Bacon Dressing

¼ C creamy Russian dressing
2 T crumbled bacon
½ C sour cream

Blend ingredients. Makes 1 cup.

Blue Velvet Dressing

1 envelope blue cheese dressing mix
2 T milk
3 T dry sherry
1 C sour cream

Combine ingredients and blend well. Makes about 1 1/3 cups.

Cottage Cheese Dressing

1 envelope garlic French dressing mix
2 T water
2 T vinegar
2/3 C small curd cottage cheese

Dissolve dressing mix in water and vinegar. Blend mixture with cottage cheese. Makes 1 cup.

Tomato Juice Italian Dressing

1 envelope Italian dressing mix
2 T water
¼ C wine vinegar
¼ C salad oil
1¼ C tomato juice

Blend ingredients. Makes 2 cups.

* * * * *

READY-TO-SERVE
PACKAGED AND CANNED
ADDITIONS TO A TOSSED SALAD

Note: add crisp ingredients just before serving.

Toasted sunflower kernels
Mexican pepitas
Walnuts, salted or unsalted
Pecans, salted or unsalted
Cashews, salted or unsalted
Almonds, salted or unsalted
Pistachios, salted or unsalted
Peanuts, dry-roasted or regular
Macadamia nuts, sliced
Canned bacon crisps
Imitation bacon bits
Canned French fried onions
Canned shoe-string potatoes
Corn chips
Cheese curls
Pretzel pieces
Other snack products
Seasoned croutons
Seasoned stuffing mix
Stuffed olives, whole or sliced
Pimiento, sliced or chopped
Salad peppers (peperoncini)

Tiny smoked oysters
Sardines
Caviar
Anchovies
Minced clams
Small frozen cooked shrimp
Pickle chips
Chutney
Pickle relish
Corn relish
Capers
Frozen chopped chives
Frozen minced onions
Canned tomatoes, wedge-style
Mushrooms, sliced or whole
Marinated mushrooms
Bean sprouts
Chinese vegetables
Water chestnuts, sliced
Canned artichokes
Marinated artichokes
Canned garbanzos, rinsed
Canned kidney beans, rinsed

Chapter 8

Breads

Bread
Rolls and Biscuits
Quick Breads and Muffins

Hot breads add a special quality of mouth-watering fragrance to a meal, and according to one school of thought they should be served always at two particular kinds of meals—dinner or luncheon parties and family meals when leftovers are being served. In the latter instance, the serving of hot bread never fails to create the happy illusion of fancier fare.

* * * * *

BREAD

Herb Batter Bread

1 pkg. (13¾ oz.) hot roll mix
¾ C warm water
2 eggs
1¼ t onion salt
1 t Italian seasoning
1 can (3½ oz.) French fried onions

In a large mixing bowl sprinkle yeast (found in mix package) over water and stir to dissolve. Blend in eggs. Add remaining ingredients and beat 50 strokes. Pour into greased 2-qt. casserole or 5 x 9-inch loaf pan, cover and let rise until double in size. Bake at 375° F. for 30 minutes. Remove from pan immediately to cool. Serves 8.

Holiday Onion Braid

2 pkgs. hot roll mix
2 envelopes onion soup mix
1 egg yolk
1 T water

Prepare roll mix according to directions, adding soup mix with the flour. Let dough rise, knead on floury surface until smooth. Divide in thirds, shaping in three 12-inch smooth, rounded lengths. Braid, sealing ends, and place on greased cookie sheet. Brush with mixture of egg yolk and water, let rise until double in size. Bake in 400° F. oven until deep, golden brown, about 30 minutes. Serves 16.

Barbecue Bread

1 loaf French or Italian bread
½ C butter, softened
Barbecue spice or salad seasoning to taste
Parmesan cheese to taste

Slice bread in ½-inch slices. Spread both sides of bread slices with butter. Sprinkle slices with spice and cheese. Reassemble loaf, wrap in foil and bake 10 minutes at 400° F. Serves 8.

Sesame Bread

2 cans refrigerator biscuits
1 egg white
2 T Sesame seeds
Garlic butter

Stand biscuits on edge on ungreased cookie sheet. Lightly press together and shape ends to form a long 14-inch loaf. Brush with egg white that has been lightly beaten, then sprinkle with sesame seeds. Bake 30 to 40 minutes at 350° F., or until deep brown. When cool slice almost to bottom crust, coat slice with garlic butter or other mixture. Wrap in foil and bake for 10 minutes at 400° F. Serves 6.

111

Garlic Bread

1 loaf French bread
1 jar (4 oz.) garlic spread
½ C oil
Grated Parmesan cheese to taste

Cut bread in slices without cutting through bottom crust. Combine and heat garlic spread and oil. Coat bread slices with mixture. Sprinkle top of loaf with Parmesan cheese. Toast under broiler until brown. Serves 8.

Spiced Bread

1 loaf French bread
½ C butter
1 t prepared mustard
2 t frozen chopped chives

Cut bread in slices without cutting through bottom crust. Melt butter and blend in mustard and chives. Brush this mixture on the top and sides of the bread slices and heat in the oven 10 minutes at 400° F. Serves 8.

Herb Loaf

¼ C butter, softened
½ t instant minced onion
¼ t caraway seed
½ t Italian seasoning
2 T instant chopped parsley
2 cans butterflake dinner rolls

Combine butter and seasonings and spread each section of dough (36 in all) with mixture. Stand on edge in 2 rows in greased bread pan (5 x 9 inches). Bake 30 to 35 minutes at 375° F. Serves 8.

Onion Loaf

1 loaf (1 lb.) frozen bread dough
½ C frozen minced onions
2 T butter

Allow dough to thaw. Punch down and roll out the dough to 10 x 12 inches on a floured surface. Sauté onions in butter until golden; cool. Spread onions and butter on dough and roll up from the shortest side. Pinch seams to seal. Place in a 5 x 9-inch greased bread pan and let rise until double. Bake as directed on bread package. Serves 8.

* * * * *

ROLLS AND BISCUITS

Salt Sticks

1 pkg. refrigerator biscuits
2 T butter, melted
Coarsely ground salt to taste
Sesame seeds to taste

Roll each biscuit into a 5-inch rope. Brush with butter, sprinkle with coarse salt and sesame seeds. Bake on an ungreased baking sheet 10 to 12 minutes in a 375° F. oven. Makes 10 sticks.

Miniaturizing refrigerator biscuits and rolls is an effective device for increasing variety. Try these easy techniques.

Cheese Crescents

1 pkg. refrigerator crescent rolls, prepared as directed
1 egg, slightly beaten
¼ C grated Parmesan cheese

Just before baking rolls, brush with beaten egg and sprinkle with cheese. Makes 8 rolls.

Garlic Sticks

6 wiener buns
½ C butter, melted
½ t garlic salt
¼ C Parmesan cheese
Poppy seeds or sesame seeds to taste

Cut wiener buns in quarters lengthwise. Combine butter and garlic salt; brush sides of buns with mixture. Sprinkle with Parmesan cheese and seeds. Toast in a 450° F. oven for 8 minutes. Makes 24 sticks

Onion Biscuits

1 pkg. refrigerator biscuits
2 T melted butter
2 T instant minced onion

Arrange biscuits on ungreased sheet. Press center of each biscuit with a teaspoon to make a depression. Fill with a mixture of onion and melted butter. Bake 8 to 10 minutes at 450° F. Makes 10.

Onion Crescents

1 pkg. refrigerator crescent rolls
1 envelope onion soup mix
1/3 C butter, softened

Before rolling up individual rolls, spread mixture of soup mix and butter on each triangle. Proceed as directed. Makes 8.

Onion Rolls

Follow the directions for Onion Biscuits, substituting butterflake rolls (yeast dough) for the biscuits. Use ½-inch sections for each roll. Bake as directed on butterflake roll package. Makes 18 small rolls.

Tiny Fan-Tan Rolls

Use 1 pkg. refrigerator butterflake rolls. Separate in·18 sections. Snip each section in two and bake in tiny muffin pans. Makes 18 small fan-tans. Use this method with flaky refrigerator biscuits, too. Serves 6.

Butter Fingers

2 pkgs. refrigerator flaky biscuits
¾ C butter

Cut each biscuit in half. Form a 2½-inch stick-like shape by rolling between your palms. Melt butter in a 9 x 13-inch baking pan. Roll strips in butter, coating them completely. Arrange in 3 long rows. Bake 15 minutes at 450° F. Serve immediately. Serves 8.

Miniature Crescents

Use 1 pkg. refrigerator crescents. Cut each triangle of dough in two smaller triangles. Roll up and bake as directed. Makes 16 small crescents. Serves 6 to 8.

* * * * *

QUICK BREADS AND MUFFINS

Many marvelously tasting mixes are all but impossible to improve. One of my favorites is a corn bread mix that beats any homemade recipe I've ever used, and the ingredients for one batch can be both measured and mixed in a two cup or four cup measuring container. I rarely alter the mix but that is a personal preference and there are many excellent variations. Here are a few of the best.

Corn-Corn Muffins

1 pkg. (8½ oz.) corn bread mix, prepared as directed
½ C whole kernel corn

Stir corn into prepared mix and bake as directed. Makes 12 2½-inch muffins.

Carnival Corn Bread

1 T frozen chopped chives
1 T chopped pimiento
¼ t thyme
1 pkg. (8½ oz.) corn muffin mix

Add chives, pimiento and thyme to dry mix and prepare as directed. Follow package directions for baking time and temperature. Makes 10 2½-inch muffins.

Peanut Muffins

1 pkg. (8½ oz.) corn muffin mix, prepared as directed
1/3 C salted peanuts

Stir peanuts into prepared mixture and bake as directed. Makes 11 2½-inch muffins.

Banana Nut Bread

1 pkg. white cake mix, 2 layer size
1 t baking soda
½ C milk
1 egg
1 C mashed banana
½ C chopped nuts

Blend all ingredients except nuts. Beat 2 minutes, stir in nuts. Pour into 2 greased 9 x 5-inch bread pans. Bake 35 to 40 minutes at 350° F. Cool 10 to 15 minutes before removing from pans. Serves 16.

Crunch Bread

1 pkg. (6 oz.) bran muffin mix
1 pkg. (8 oz.) honey date muffin mix
2 eggs
2 T oil
⅞ C milk
½ C chopped pecans

116

Combine all ingredients and stir until well blended. (To get an easy, accurate milk measure pour the 2 T of oil into a 1 cup measure and add enough milk to make 1 cup.) Line the bottom of a 5 x 9-inch greased bread pan with wax paper. Add the batter and bake 40 minutes at 350° F. Remove bread from pan and cool on a rack. Serves 8.

Cheese Corn Bread

1 pkg. (8½ oz.) corn muffin mix, prepared as directed
1 t instant minced onion
½ C shredded Cheddar cheese

Add onions and cheese to prepared muffin mix. Bake as directed in an 8-inch square greased baking pan. Serves 6.

Raisin Pecan Corn Bread or Muffins

1 pkg. (8½ oz.) corn muffin mix, prepared as directed
2 T chopped pecans
2 T raisins

Stir nuts and raisins into prepared mixture and bake as directed. Makes 11 2½-inch muffins.

Date-Filled Bran Muffins

1 pkg. (6 oz.) bran muffin mix
1/3 C date cake and pastry filling (approx.)

Prepare muffins as directed. Fill muffin tins half full; place a heaping teaspoonful of date filling in the center of each muffin. Bake as directed. Makes 8 (2½-inch) muffins.

For additional quick breads, see:
Cinnamon Nut Loaf, p. 151
Christmas Fruit Loaf, p. 150
Yorkshire Pudding, p. 99

Chapter 9

Desserts

Here begins the longest chapter in the book and the most enjoyable if your family suffers from that not uncommon affliction, sweet tooth.

According to the head of our household, a dessertless meal is like a mystery story with the last chapter missing. And, as far as he's concerned, dessert is neither a low calorie pudding nor the passing of the fruit bowl. A proper dessert, by his definition, contains no less than 500 calories per serving, is chocolate flavored, and possesses such ambrosial qualities that he couldn't possibly pass up a second helping. Feed him sweets and you give him love!

* * * * *

CAKES

Chocolate Coffee Torte

1 pkg. (17 oz.) brownie mix
1 C chopped walnuts
½ C light brown sugar
2 t instant coffee powder
2 envelopes whipped topping mix, prepared as directed

118

Prepare brownie mix according to cake-type directions. Stir in nuts. Bake in 2 9-inch cake pans. Beat brown sugar and coffee powder into prepared topping. Split cooled layers horizontally. Put the four layers together with topping mixture, leaving top unfrosted. Chill at least 1 hour before serving. Serves 12 to 16.

Fruit Cake

1 pkg. (1 lb.) nut bread mix (or date bread mix)
1 t pumpkin pie spice
1 egg
1 C orange juice
1½ C preserved fruit
¾ C chopped dates*
¾ C raisins
¾ C chopped walnuts or pecans (optional)

Combine first four ingredients. Stir until dry particles are moistened. Stir in fruit, dates, raisins, and nuts. Pour mixture into a greased baking pan (4½ x 13-inch) which has been lined with brown paper. Bake 1 hour at 350° F. To decorate, remove cake from oven after 50 minutes. Brush top of cake with beaten egg white and decorate with preserved cherry halves. Return to oven and bake 10 minutes more. Serves 18.

* When using date bread mix, substitute chopped walnuts for the dates.

High Sour Cream Cake

1 pkg. white, chocolate or yellow cake mix (2 layer size)
3 eggs
1 C sour cream
1 t baking soda
¼ C water

Combine all ingredients and beat with electric mixer 2 minutes. Pour into a 10-inch greased tube pan and bake 45 minutes at 350° F. Frost with ready-to-eat lemon frosting. Serves 12.

Real Apple Strudel

1 pkg. (2 oz.) frozen strudel leaves * (use 2 leaves)
2 T butter, melted
1 C vanilla wafer or cake crumbs

Dampen a 2 ft. by 3 ft. cotton cloth and spread it on your work area. Unfold 2 thawed, 18-inch square strudel leaves on the damp cloth, overlapping them slightly to form an 18 x 30-inch rectangle (approximately). Brush pastry with melted butter (use a pastry brush) and sprinkle with crumbs. Don't worry about small tears in this delicate pastry, they don't matter. Spread apple filling (below) in a three inch strip across one end (short side) of pastry. Use the damp cloth, not your fingers, to roll up the strudel and to transfer it to a greased cookie sheet. Tuck in the ends. Bake 35 minutes at 350° F. Serves 6.

* A strudel leaf is a paper thin square of strudel dough.

Apple Filling

4 C sliced cooking apples
½ C sugar
¼ C raisins
¼ C chopped pecans
½ t cinamon

Mix all ingredients and proceed as above.

Cream Puffs

This recipe has one advantage over the standard cream puff recipe—you don't measure any flour.

1 stick pie crust mix, crumbled
2/3 C water
2 eggs

Bring water to a boil in a small saucepan. Add crumbled pie crust mix and stir vigorously until pastry forms a ball and leaves the side of the pan. Remove from heat. Beat in eggs with an electric mixer. Drop by the spoonful on a greased cookie sheet. Bake 30 minutes at 400° F. Turn off heat and remove puffs 5 minutes later. Allow puffs to cool before filling. To fill use Cream Puff Filling p. 129. Slice off the top of each puff, spoon in filling and replace tops. Dust with confectioners' sugar. Makes 12 2½-inch puffs.

Chocolate Eclairs

Shape cream puff dough (above) in 3-inch ribbons; bake as directed above. When cool, fill with prepared vanilla pudding and pie filling mix and frost with ready to eat chocolate frosting. Makes 12.

Meringue Cake

The frosting is baked on the cake.

1 pkg. Swiss style, or any other chocolate cake mix, 2 layer size
2 eggs, separated
1 pkg. coconut almond frosting mix, prepared as directed

Prepare cake mix as directed, but add 2 additional egg yolks. Pour into a greased and floured 9 x 13-inch cake pan. Beat egg whites to stiff peaks and fold into prepared frosting. Spoon over cake batter. Bake 35 minutes at 350° F. Cool before serving. Serves 12.

Coconut-Pecan Cheese Cake

1 frozen cheese cake, purchased
1 pkg. coconut pecan frosting mix, prepared as directed

Remove frozen cheese cake from pan and place on plate. Prepare frosting mix as directed and spread on top of frozen cake. Serve when cake has thawed (about 45 minutes at room temperature). Serves 8.

Lord Baltimore Cake

Prepare 2 9-inch chocolate cake layers. Frost as directed with Lord Baltimore Frosting below. Serves 12.

Lord Baltimore Filling and Frosting

2 pkgs. (5¼ oz. each) fluffy white frosting mix, prepared
    as directed
½ C crushed dry macaroons
¼ C chopped pecans
¼ C chopped almonds
12 candied cherries, cut in quarters
1 T sherry

To 1 C of prepared frosting add remaining ingredients. Mix well. Use as filling between layers. Frost cake with remaining frosting. Frosts 2 9-inch layers.

Easy Sachertorte

The original Sachertorte is made with a spiced chocolate cake and apricot jam. In this recipe the apricot filling contains the spices the cake lacks. It all adds up to the same good taste.

1 pkg. chocolate cake mix, 2 layer size
1 can (12 oz.) apricot cake and pastry filling
1 can (21 oz.) chocolate frosting

Bake cake in 2 9-inch pans according to package directions. When cool, split layers to make 4 thin layers. Spread 3 of these layers with 1/3 C frosting then ½ C apricot filling. Stack layers on a serving plate. Top with the plain layer. Frost sides and top with a thin layer of remaining frosting. Chill before cutting in small wedges. This is a rich one. Serves 12 to 16.

Chocolate Spice Torte

12 lady fingers, split
½ C orange marmalade
1 to 2 T water
2 pkgs. chocolate fudge whipped dessert mix
½ t cinnamon
1 envelope whipped topping mix, prepared as directed

Line a 9 x 5-inch loaf pan with waxed paper. Arrange lady fingers on bottom and sides of pan (reserving 5 for second layer.) Stir marmalade and water together until spreading consistency. Combine cinnamon and dessert mix; prepare as directed. Spread bottom layer of lady fingers with half of marmalade. Top with half of chocolate mixture. Arrange remaining lady fingers (spread with marmalade) on top. Add remaining chocolate mixture. Chill 2 hours. Top with prepared whipped topping.

Cherry Crisp

1 can (22 oz.) cherry pie filling (or other fruit pie filling)
1 pkg. (9 oz.) white cake mix (1 layer size)
¼ C butter, melted
½ C slivered almonds

Pour pie filling into an 8-inch square baking pan. Sprinkle dry cake mix evenly over fruit. Dribble melted butter over all and top with nuts. Bake 45 minutes at 350° F. Serve hot or cold, topped with whipped cream or ice cream. Serves 6 to 9.

Basic Lemon Cheese Cake

1 pkg. instant lemon pudding mix
1 pkg. (8 oz.) cream cheese, softened
1 8-inch graham cracker crust

Prepare instant pudding as directed, but blend softened cheese with milk before stirring in pudding. Pour into pie shell and chill 1 hour. Serves 6.

Meringue Date Cake

1 pkg. date bar mix
½ C hot water
2 eggs
1 t baking powder
¼ C current or apple jelly
1 pkg. fluffy white frosting mix, prepared as directed
2 T sugar

Blend date filling with water. Stir in crumbly mix, eggs and baking powder. Pour into an 8-inch square greased baking pan. Bake 30 minutes at 375° F. Spread jelly on hot cake. Top with mixture of prepared frosting mix and sugar, beaten until very stiff. Be sure frosting touches sides of pan. Return to oven and bake 10 minutes at 400° F. Serves 9.

Apple Ginger Cake

1 pkg. (13 oz.) gingerbread mix
½ C water
1 C applesauce
¼ C chopped nuts
¼ C raisins
1 can (21 oz.) apple pie filling

Combine gingerbread mix, water and applesauce. Beat 2 minutes; add nuts. Spread apple pie filling and raisins in a 9-inch square greased baking pan. Top with gingerbread mixture. Bake 30 minutes at 375° F. Remove from oven and invert cake on serving rack. Serve warm or cold with a dollop of whipped cream. Serves 9.

Marble Cake

1 pkg. yellow or white cake mix (2 layer size)
1 envelope whipped topping mix
4 eggs
1 C water
1 envelope (1 oz.) liquid baking chocolate

Blend all ingredients except chocolate and beat with a mixer 4 minutes. Pour all but 2 cups of batter into a greased 10-inch tube pan. Stir chocolate into remaining batter. Spoon chocolate batter into tube pan; marbelize by running a knife through the batters. Bake 45 minutes at 350° F. Cool in pan 10 minutes before removing to cool on rack. Frost with Glossy Chocolate Frosting, p. 129. Serves 12.

Angel Torte

1 pkg. chocolate pudding and pie filling mix
1 C milk
½ C sour cream
9- or 10-inch angel food cake, purchased
1 C heavy cream, whipped
3 T confectioners' sugar
Shaved chocolate

Combine pudding mix with milk and cook until mixture boils. Cool slightly and stir in sour cream. Chill thoroughly. Split angel food cake in 2 or 3 layers; spread chocolate mixture between layers. Cover top and sides of cake with whipped cream, sweetened with confectioners' sugar and garnish with shaved chocolate. Serves 10.

Trifle

8 sponge cake dessert cups
8 t frozen orange juice concentrate
¼ t almond extract, optional
1 can vanilla pudding
½ C raspberry preserves
¼ C almonds, sliced and toasted

Place dessert cups on individual plates. Spoon 1 t orange concentrate over each. Stir almond extract into pudding. When ready to serve place 1 T preserves in bottom of each cup, top with ¼ C pudding and sprinkle with almonds. Serves 8.

Karen's Brandied Peach Cheese Cake

1 pkg. (8 oz.) cream cheese, softened
1¾ C milk
¼ C cognac or other brandy
1 pkg. instant vanilla pudding mix
1 8-inch graham cracker crust
1 pkg. (10 oz.) frozen peaches, thawed and drained
¼ C current jelly
2 t (additional) cognac

Stir cream cheese until soft; blend in ½ C milk. Add remaining milk, cognac and pudding mix. Beat slowly just until well mixed. Pour into crust. Chill 1 hour. Arrange peach slices attractively on cheese filling. Heat jelly and additional cognac together. Pour over peach slices. Chill. Serves 6.

Lazy Daisy Cake

1 pkg. yellow cake mix (2 layer size), prepared as directed
½ C butter
1 C brown sugar
1 pkg. (4 oz.) shredded coconut
1/3 C cream

Bake cake in a 9 x 13-inch baking pan. Turn out on a broiler-proof platter or leave in the pan to cool. Combine and heat remaining ingredients. Spread mixture over cake and broil until lightly brown. Serves 10 to 12.

Blueberry Pecan Loaf

1 pkg. pound cake mix
½ t cinnamon
½ t nutmeg
1/3 C white raisins
1 C fresh or frozen blueberries
Flour
1/3 C chopped pecans

Add spices to dry mix and prepare pound cake as directed. Dust raisins and blueberries with flour. Fold them with the pecans into the batter. Bake in a greased 5 x 9-inch loaf pan as directed on cake mix package. Ice with prepared lemon frosting mix or sprinkle with confectioners' sugar. Serves 10 to 12.

Lemon Ring

1 9-inch angel food cake, purchased
1 can (1 lb.) lemon pudding
2 envelopes whipped topping mix, prepared as directed
10 crushed hard lemon candies

Line a 10-inch tube pan with wax paper. Tear angel food cake into bite-size pieces after removing crusts, Fold lemon pudding into whipped topping along with the candy. Fill pan with alternate layers of lemon mixture and cake. Cover and refrigerate overnight. Unmold and garnish with additional crushed lemon candy if desired. Serves 10.

Burnt Sugar Cake

3 T granulated sugar
1 pkg. white or yellow cake mix (2 layer size)

Heat sugar in a small skillet over high heat, stirring constantly with a wooden spoon until melted. Lower the heat and stir until dark brown. Cool slightly. Carefully stir in ½ C of (heated) liquid called for in cake mix directions. Stir until sugar dissolves. Cool. Measure and add water, if necessary, to make ½ cup of liquid. Prepare cake mix as directed substituting burnt sugar syrup for ½ C liquid. Frost with vanilla or caramel frosting. Serves 10.

Brownie Fudge Pudding

1 pkg. (17 oz.) brownie mix
½ C chopped nuts
¾ C granulated sugar
¾ C brown sugar
1/3 C cocoa
1¼ C cold coffee

Prepare brownie mix according to cake-type directions. Stir in nuts. Pour into greased 9 x 13-inch pan. Sprinkle with mixture of sugars and cocoa. Dribble coffee over all. Bake as directed on package. Serve warm, pudding side up, topped with ice cream or whipped cream, if desired. Serves 12.

Letty's Pound Cake

1 pkg. yellow cake mix (2 layer size)
1 pkg. (3 oz.) instant lemon pudding mix
½ C oil
1 C milk
4 eggs
Dash mace
Confectioners' sugar

Combine all ingredients but sugar and beat with an electric mixer 2 minutes. Bake in a greased 10-inch tube pan 1 hour at 350° F. When cool sprinkle with confectioners' sugar. Serves 12.

Cinnamon Torte

1 box (5¼ oz.) fluffy white frosting mix, prepared as directed
1 C crushed cinnamon graham crackers
1 t vanilla
½ C flaky coconut
½ C chopped pecans

Fold remaining ingredients into prepared frosting mix. Pile lightly in 9-inch greased pie plate. Bake 30 minutes at

350° F. To serve, cut in wedges and top with cinnamon ice cream. Serves 6.

* * * * *

FROSTINGS AND FILLINGS

Cream Puff Filling

1 can (1 lb.) vanilla pudding
2 T Cointreau
½ C heavy cream, whipped

Blend pudding and Cointreau. Fold in whipped cream and chill. Fills 12 cream puffs.

Mint Chocolate Blender Icing

1 C sugar
1 can (6 oz.) evaporated milk
4 envelopes (1 oz. each) liquid baking chocolate
½ t mint flavoring
Dash salt

Pour sugar in blender, cover, and process at high speed. Add remaining ingredients and blend at high speed until thick. Covers a 9-inch layer cake.

Glossy Chocolate Frosting

½ C evaporated milk
Dash salt
1 pkg. (6 oz.) chocolate chips
1 t vanilla

Combine milk and salt. Bring just to a boil over medium heat. Add chocolate chips and vanilla. Stir until chocolate melts and mixture is smooth. Cool until thick enough to spread. Frosts a 9x13-inch cake or 2 8-inch layers.

Chocolate Creme Frosting

1 bowl (4½ oz.) non-dairy whipped topping
1 envelope (1 oz.) liquid baking chocolate

Squeeze chocolate from envelope directly into bowl of whipped topping. Stir until well blended. Frosts a 9x13-inch cake.

Chocolate Sour Cream Filling

1 pkg. chocolate pudding and pie filling
1 C milk
½ C sour cream

Combine pudding mix with milk and cook just until mixture bubbles. Cool slightly and stir in sour cream. Chill. Fills 2 9-inch layers.

Basic Instant Frosting

1 envelope whipped topping mix
1½ C cold milk
1 pkg. instant pudding mix, any flavor

Blend all ingredients in a small deep bowl. Beat with electric mixer until mixture forms soft peaks (4 to 6 minutes). Frosts 2 8-inch layers.

Ellie's Chocolate Whipping Cream Frosting

1 pkg. instant chocolate pudding mix
1 C milk
1 C heavy cream (½ pint)

Combine ingredients and beat until fluffy. Use as a filling or frosting. Covers a 10-inch angel cake.

Pudding Fillings

Use canned pudding, prepared pudding and pie filling mix, or instant pudding mixes between cake layers.

Lemon Cream Frosting

1 pkg. (9 oz.) non-dairy whipped topping
1 can (1 lb.) lemon pudding

Empty topping into a large bowl and stir in the pudding. This will frost generously (½ inch thick) a 10-inch double layer cake.

Fruit Fillings

Use the wide variety of canned cake and pie fillings between cake layers. Each can contains sufficient filling to cover 2 or 3 9-inch layers.

For additional fruit fillings, see:
Lord Baltimore Filling and Frosting, p. 122

Lord Baltimore Filling and Frosting, p. 122

* * * * *

COOKIES AND BARS

Peanut Butter Cookies

Here is the timesaver counterpart of the best standard peanut butter cookie recipe.

¼ C butter or margarine, softened
½ C brown sugar
1 egg
1 jar (12 oz.) chunk-style peanut butter
1 pkg. (9 oz.) yellow cake mix

Combine ingredients in order given, blending completely after each addition. Shape into 1-inch balls. Flatten with a fork on an ungreased cookie sheet. Bake 10 minutes at 350° F. Makes 60 cookies.

Krispie Bars #1

These are a popular snack with the Junior High crowd and a favorite recipe of blossoming cooks.

1 pkg. (6 oz.) butterscotch bits
½ C peanut butter
3 C Rice Krispies

Melt butterscotch bits and peanut butter in top of double boiler. Stir in cereal. Press into a 9-inch square greased pan. Cut into 16 squares.

Krispie Bars #2

1 pkg. (6 oz.) chocolate chips
1/3 C peanut butter
4 C Coco Rice Krispies

Melt chips and peanut butter. Follow directions above.

Krispie Bars #3

½ lb. marshmallows
¼ C butter
5 C Rice Krispies

Melt marshamallow and butter. Follow directions above.

Christmas Cookies

1 roll (18 oz.) refrigerator sugar cookies
Red and green colored sugar
Red and green candied cherries

Slice cookie roll in half lengthwise. Reshape each segment into a cylinder. Roll one cyilnder in red colored sugar, slice according to directions. Dot center of each cookie with half a green candied cherry. Reverse colors for second roll. Bake as directed. Makes 60 2-inch cookies.

Coconut Bars

1 pkg. (9 oz.) white cake mix, 1 layer size
½ C coconut, flake style
¼ C brown sugar
¼ C rolled oats
3 T water
1 egg
¼ C sugar
¼ C chopped walnuts

Measure all but last two ingredients into a mixing bowl. Stir until well blended. Spread in a greased 9-inch square baking pan. Sprinkle with mixture of sugar and chopped walnuts. Bake 25 minutes in a 350° F. oven. Serve hot or cold. Makes 15 2 x 3-inch bars.

Chocolate Crinkle Cookies

1 pkg. (17 oz.) brownie mix, prepared as directed
Confectioners' sugar

Chill prepared brownie mix several hours or overnight. Drop small spoonfuls of dough into confectioners' sugar. Roll in sugar while shaping in ball. Place 2-inches apart on greased cookie sheet. Bake 8 minutes at 350° F. Makes 48 cookies.

Date Dainties

1 pkg. (6 oz.) chocolate chips
2 T butter
2 T evaporated milk
1 can (8 oz.) date and nut roll
1 C chopped nuts

Combine and melt chocolate chips, butter and milk in a double boiler. Cut date-nut roll in 4 slices; cut each slice into 9 cubes. Dip each cube in the chocolate mixture and roll in nuts. Chill on waxed paper to set. Makes 36 dainties.

Kolachy

2 pkgs. (3 oz. each) cream cheese
2 sticks pie crust mix
2 T sugar
½ can prune, apricot or date cake and pastry filling
Confectioners' sugar

Beat cream cheese to soften; add pie crust mix and sugar. Mix thoroughly. Chill 1 hour. Roll out to ¼-inch thickness on a floured surface. Cut in 3-inch rounds. Place on ungreased cookie sheet, indent center with spoon and fill with about 1 T fruit filling. Bake at 350° F. for 12 minutes or until edges are slightly brown. When cool, sprinkle with confectioners' sugar. Makes 24 cookies.

Super Brownies For Chocolate Lovers

1 pkg. (17 oz.) brownie mix
1 pkg. (6 oz.) mint chocolate chips
1 can ready-to-eat fudge frosting

Prepare brownie mix as directed, but stir in chocolate chips. Bake as directed in a 9 x 13-inch pan. When cool, frost with fudge frosting. Cut in 20 squares.

Basic Cake Mix Cookies

1 pkg. cake mix, 2 layer size
½ C soft shortening or butter (1 stick)
1 T water
2 eggs
Optional: 1 C chopped nuts, flaky coconut, or chocolate or
    butterscotch bits.

Empty half of cake mix into bowl and add remaining ingredients. Blend well. Add balance of cake mix and beat until smooth. Blend in optional ingredients. Drop by teaspoonfuls on greased cookie sheets. Bake 10 to 12 minutes at 375° F. Makes 60 cookies.

Meringue Kisses

1 pkg. fluffy white frosting mix (5¼ oz.)
¼ C sugar
1½ C coconut

Prepare frosting mix as directed on package, but reduce boiling water to 1/3 cup. After beating 5 minutes, gradually beat in ¼ cup sugar. Fold in coconut. Drop by small spoonfuls on a greased and floured cookie sheet. Bake 1 hour at 225° F. Makes 36.

Praline Cookies

24 graham crackers
1 C butter (2 sticks)
1 C brown sugar
1 C chopped pecans

Arrange crackers on an ungreased cookie sheet. Heat butter and brown sugar to boiling, add pecans. Pour mixture over crackers. Spread to cover. Bake 10 minutes at 350° F. Cut crackers in half while still hot. Makes 48 cookies.

Rum Balls

2 C crushed vanilla wafers
Dash salt
1 C sifted confectioners' sugar
½ C nut filling (solo type)
1 t rum flavoring
Confectioners' sugar

Combine wafers, salt and sugar. Stir in nut filling and rum flavoring. Mix thoroughly. Form ¾-inch balls, roll in confectioners' sugar. Makes 30 balls.

Applesauce Cookies

1 pkg. spice cake mix (2 layers)
½ C oil
½ C applesauce
1 egg
1½ C raisins
1 can lemon ready-to-eat frosting

Combine all ingredients except frosting, and mix well. Drop from a teaspoon onto an ungreased cookie sheet. Bake 12 to 15 minutes at 350° F. Frost when cool. Makes 60 cookies.

Ginger Cookies

1 pkg. (13½ oz.) gingerbread mix
1/3 C lukewarm water

Add water to gingerbread mix and mix until smooth. Chill 2 hours. Roll out dough to 1/8-inch thickness and cut with cookie cutter. Keep unused dough refrigerated as you work. Place cookies on a greased cookie sheet. Bake 8 to 10 minutes at 375° F. Makes 36 cookies.

Date Bars

1 pkg. (8 oz.) honey-date muffin mix
1 egg
2 T milk
½ stick butter, softened (¼ C)
1 pkg. (8 oz.) diced dates (1 C)
½ C chopped pecans (optional)

Blend first four ingredients thoroughly; add dates and nuts. Spread in a greased 8-inch square baking pan. Bake 30 minutes at 350° F. Cool in pan, cut into 18 bars and sprinkle with confectioners' sugar. Makes 18 bars.

1 pkg. pound cake mix (17 oz.)
4 oz. preserved fruit, finely diced

Prepare pound cake as directed, but reduce milk to ½ C
(or two thirds of required amount of liquid). Fold in preserved fruit. Drop by very small spoonfuls on a greased
cookie sheet, allowing room for spreading. Bake 10 minutes at 350° F. Makes 12 dozen cookies.

* * * * *

PIES, CRUSTS AND THINGS TO DO WITH READY-TO-BAKE FROZEN PIES

Toasted Coconut Custard Pie

1½ C coconut
1 8-inch pie shell
1 pkg. real egg custard mix
1¾ C lukewarm milk
Cinnamon to taste

Set aside ½ C coconut. Place remaining 1 C coconut in
bottom of unbaked pie shell. Dissolve custard mix in milk
and pour into pie shell. Sprinkle with cinnamon. Bake 10
minutes at 450° F. Reduce heat and bake 30 minutes
longer at 350° F. Sprinkle remaining coconut on the pie
during the last 10 minutes of baking. It should toast to a
golden brown. Cool before cutting. Serves 6.

Apricot Mince Pie

1 can (1 lb.) mincemeat
1 can (12 oz.) apricot cake and pastry filling
1 9-inch top and bottom crust (see Double Crust, p. 144)

Combine mincemeat and apricot filling. Pour into pie shell,
cover with top crust. Bake 50 minutes at 425° F. Serves 6.

Sour Cream Lemon Chiffon Pie

1 can (6 oz.) frozen lemonade concentrate
1 envelope (1 oz.) unflavored gelatin
4 eggs, separated
Dash salt
½ C sugar
1 C sour cream
1 9-inch baked pie shell

Allow lemonade to thaw slightly, pour into a saucepan, and sprinkle with gelatin. Let stand to soften. Beat egg yolks with a dash of salt; add to lemonade mixture. Heat over low heat until gelatin is dissolved. Chill in refrigerator until mixture mounds. Beat egg whites until foamy. Beat in sugar gradually until soft peaks form. Fold in lemon mixture and most of sour cream (reserve a bit for garnish). Spoon into a 9-inch baked pie shell. Chill 2 hours or until set. Serves 8.

Refrigerator Pumpkin Pie

1 pkg. lemon or vanilla whipped dessert mix
¼ C sugar
1 t pumpkin pie spice
½ C cold milk
¼ C cold water
1 C pumpkin
1 8- or 9-inch gingersnap crust

Combine all ingredients except pumpkin and pie crust in a deep, narrow bowl. Whip 3 minutes. Stir in pumpkin. Pour into a Gingersnap Crust, p. 144 or an 8- or 9-inch baked pie shell. Chill at least 3 hours. Serves 6.

Appledate Pie

1 pkg. date bar mix, prepared as directed
2 cans (21 oz. each) apple pie filling
2 9-inch frozen pie shells

Prepare the two mixtures (dates and crumbs) of the date bar mix. Stir the apple pie filling into the date mixture. Spoon half the mixture into each unbaked pie shell. Top with crumb mixture and bake 30 minutes at 400° F., until crumb topping is golden brown. Serves 12.

Blueberry Cobbler

1 pkg. refrigerator blueberry turnover pastries
1 can (21 oz.) blueberry pie filling
1 T lemon juice
Sugar and cinnamon to taste

Following directions on turnover pastry box, make 2 turnovers. Wrap and freeze for another day. Store icing in the refrigerator. Pour pie filling into 8 x 12-inch baking pan. Stir in remaining turnover filling and lemon juice. Heat 10 minutes at 400° F. Remove from oven and arrange 6 squares of dough on top of fruit. Sprinkle with sugar and cinnamon mixture. Bake 13 minutes at 400° F. or until pastry browns. Serves 6.

Lime Pistachio Chiffon Pie

1 can (6 oz.) frozen limeade concentrate, thawed
1 envelope (1 oz.) unflavored gelatin
1 pkg. fluffy white frosting mix, prepared as directed
2 to 3 drops green food coloring
1 envelope whipped topping mix, prepared as directed
1/3 C chopped pistachio nuts
1 9-inch baked pie shell

Stir gelatin into thawed limeade. Heat until dissolved; cool. Add coloring to prepared frosting mix. Beat limeade mixture into prepared whipped topping. Fold this mixture and nuts into frosting. Turn into a 9-inch baked pie shell. Chill 30 to 60 minutes. Serve this pie in small wedges—it's very rich. Serves 8.

Chocolate Silk Pie

½ C butter (1 stick)
1 C confectioners' sugar
2 envelopes (1 oz. each) liquid baking chocolate
2 eggs
¼ t peppermint extract
1 t vanilla extract
1 8-inch baked pie shell

Cream butter, add sugar, and beat until fluffy. Beat in chocolate, eggs (one at a time), and extracts. Spread attractively in an 8-inch baked pie shell and refrigerate 6 hours. Serve small portions with whipped cream—it's rich. Serves 8.

Baked Pumpkin Pie

1 can (1 lb.) pumpkin
2 t pumpkin pie spice
½ C sugar
1 pkg. real egg custard
1¼ C milk
1 8- or 9-inch pie shell

Combine ingredients and pour mixture into an unbaked 8- or 9-inch pie shell. Bake 10 minutes at 425° F. Reduce heat to 350° F. and bake 50 minutes longer. Serves 6.

Date Sponge Pie

1 pkg. vanilla whipped dessert mix, prepared as directed
1 can (12 oz.) date cake and pastry filling
1 9-inch frozen pie shell, baked as directed
¼ C chopped pecans

Beat date filling into prepared dessert mix with electric mixer. Pour into cooled pie crust; sprinkle with chopped nuts. Chill 1 hour before serving. Serves 8.

Grasshopper Pie

24 marshmallows
½ C milk
¼ C green creme de menthe
2 T white creme de Cacao
1 C heavy cream, whipped
Chocolate crumb crust*

Melt marshmallows in milk over low heat. Cool. Stir in creme de menthe and creme de Cacao, and fold mixture into whipped cream. Pour into an 8-inch chocolate crumb crust and freeze. Decorate with whipped cream before serving. Serves 6 to 8.

* Use recipe for Chocolate Spice Crust, p. 145, but omit cinnamon.

Eggnog Pie

1 pkg. vanilla instant pudding
2 C canned eggnog
1 9-inch graham cracker crust
1 envelope whipped topping mix
½ t rum flavoring
Nutmeg to taste

Prepare the instant pudding as directed, substituting eggnog for milk. Chill slightly and pour into graham cracker crust. Stir rum flavoring into prepared topping. Cover pie with topping. Sprinkle nutmeg over all. Chill. Serves 6.

Rocky Road Frozen Pie

½ C salted pecans, coarsely chopped
½ C chocolate chips, chopped
1 C miniature marshmallows
1 pkg. chocolate whipped dessert mix, prepared as directed
1 8-inch baked pie shell

Fold nuts (reserving a few for garnish), chocolate chips, and marshmallows into prepared whipped dessert mix. Spoon into pre-baked pie shell. Sprinkle top with reserved nuts. Freeze at least 3 hours. Serves 6.

Hot Blueberry Crumble

1 can (21 oz.) blueberry pie filling
1 stick pie crust mix
½ C brown sugar
1 t cinnamon

Pour blueberry filling (or any pre-cooked fruit pie filling) into an 8-inch pie pan and heat in a 350° F. oven for 10 minutes. Mix pie crust mix, sugar and cinnamon with a pastry blender. Sprinkle this crumbly mixture over hot fruit and broil about 4 minutes or until golden brown. Serves 4 to 6.

Deep Dish Cherry Pie in Ramekins

½ t almond extract
Red food coloring
1 can (21 oz.) cherry pie filling
1 pkg. frozen puff pastry shells (6 shells)

Stir almond extract and a drop or 2 of red food coloring into cherry filling. Divide mixture among 6 ramekins. Thaw puff pastry shells. On a floured surface, roll out each shell to fit top of ramekin. Place a round of pastry over cherries in each ramekin. Follow directions for time and temperature on pastry shell package. Serves 6.

Apple Relish Pie

1 9-inch unbaked pie shell
¾ C toasted chopped almonds
1 pkg. (10 oz.) frozen cranberry-orange relish
1 can (21 oz.) apple pie filling

Sprinkle ¼ C almonds in bottom of unbaked pie shell. Combine relish and apple filling. Pour over almonds. Sprinkle remaining almonds over filling. Bake at 400° F. for 25 to 30 minutes. Serves 6.

Brownie Pie

1 pkg. (21 oz.) brownie mix, prepared as directed
1 C nuts, coarsely chopped
2 frozen 8- or 9-inch pie shells

Add ½ C nuts to prepared brownie mix. Pour mixture into 2 pie shells. Sprinkle remaining nuts on top. Bake 20 minutes at 350° F. The brownie mixture should be slightly underdone. Serve hot or cold with mocha ice cream. Serves 12.

PIE CRUSTS

Cheese Crust

1 stick pie crust mix
1 jar (5 oz.) sharp Old English cheese
      (processed Cheddar)

Combine pie crust mix and cheese. Roll out to fit a 10-inch pie pan. Prick bottom and sides with a fork. Bake 10 minutes at 425° F.

Pecan Pastry

1 frozen pie shell
½ C finely chopped pecans

Allow pie shell to thaw slightly. Press chopped pecans evenly into bottom and sides of crust. Bake as directed.

Sesame Seed Pastry

3 T sesame seeds
1 stick pie crust mix, prepared as directed

Toast sesame seeds in a 350° F. oven for 20 minutes. Cool and add to pie crust mixture. Roll out and bake as directed on pie crust mix package.

Double Crust

2 frozen pie shells (thaw one)

Fill one frozen shell. Remove thawed second crust from pan and place over filled shell to form top crust. Tuck top crust edge under edge of bottom crust and seal edges well.

Chocolate Chip Crust

1 ready-made graham cracker crust
½ C chocolate chips (or butterscotch chips)

Scatter chips in bottom of crust. Bake as directed.

Gingersnap Crust

1¼ C gingersnap cookie crumbs
1/3 C soft margarine or butter

Process cookies in blender for quick crumbs. Combine crumbs and butter or margarine, press firmly on bottom and sides of an 8-inch pie pan. Chill 1 hour, or bake 8 minutes at 375° F. and cool before filling.

Walnut Crunch Crust

1 stick pie crust mix
2 T brown sugar
½ C finely chopped walnuts
1 egg yolk, slightly beaten
½ t vanilla

Blend pie crust mix and sugar with a pastry blender. Stir in remaining ingredients. Press into bottom and sides of a 9-inch pie pan. Bake at 375° F. for 10 minutes or until golden.

Peanut Butter Crust

¼ C chunk-style peanut butter
¼ C margarine or butter
1½ C graham cracker crumbs
2 T sugar

Combine peanut butter and margarine; stir in crumbs and sugar. Press into a 9-inch pie pan. Chill until firm.

Coconut Crust

¼ C butter
2 C coconut, flaked or shredded
½ C chocolate chips (optional)

Melt butter in a skillet. Add coconut and sauté until light brown, stirring constantly. Press firmly on bottom and sides of an 8- or 9-inch pie pan. Cool 30 minutes before filling. When using chocolate chips, add them to coconut mixture just before pressing into pie pan.

Chocolate Spice Crust

1 C chocolate wafer crumbs
3 T sugar
¼ t cinnamon
¼ C softened butter

Combine all ingredients. Press into bottom and sides of an 8-inch pie pan. Bake 8 minutes at 375° F.

THINGS TO DO WITH A READY-TO-BAKE FROZEN PIE

Frosted Pie

Spread top crust of cooled pie with half a can of ready-to-eat frosting. Try lemon frosting on blueberry pie.

Golden Dome Pie

Sprinkle top crust with ½ C shredded Cheddar cheese 10 minutes before pie is finished baking. Continue baking until pie is done. Great with apple pie.

Sugar 'N Spice Pie

1 egg white, slightly beaten
¼ C sugar
¼ C chopped nuts
½ t cinnamon

Before baking, brush top crust with egg white. Combine remaining ingredients and sprinkle over crust. Bake as directed.

Meringue Pie

2 egg whites
Dash salt
¼ C sugar
¼ C slivered almonds

Beat egg whites with salt until foamy. Gradually beat in sugar until mixture is stiff. Heap meringue on top crust of a hot baked pie. Sprinkle with almonds. Bake at 425° F. 5 to 10 minutes or until brown. Try this one with cherry pie.

Butterscotch Layer Pie

1 pkg. (6 oz.) butterscotch bits

Scatter butterscotch bits on crust 5 minutes before pie is done. Continue baking until pie is done. Remove from oven and immediately spread melted bits in an even coating over crust.

Candy Bar Pie

1 peanut (or pecan, coconut, or almond) brittle bar

Break up brittle bar in small pieces. Sprinkle on crust 10 minutes before pie is done baking. Continue baking until pie is done and candy has melted into crust.

Fruit Sauce Pie

Pour Basic Sweet Sauce, p. 163, or Cider Sauce, p. 162, over hot pie just before serving. See Dessert Toppings, p. 160, for other sauce recipes.

* * * * *

COFFEE CAKES, SWEET ROLLS, DOUGHNUTS, ETC.

See Bread, Chapter 8, for quick breads and muffin recipes.

Swedish Cardamom Coffee Cake

1 pkg. hot roll mix, or yeast coffee cake mix
1 t crushed cardamom seed
1 egg white
2 T sugar
2 T chopped almonds

Prepare hot roll dough as directed, but add cardamom seed to batter. Let rise once, as directed. Roll dough out on floured surface in an 8 x 12-inch rectangle. Cut in three strips, lengthwise. Place strips on greased cookie sheet and braid. Pinch ends together and tuck under. Let rise until double in size, about 30 minutes. Brush with beaten egg white and sprinkle with mixture of sugar and nuts. Bake 25 minutes at 350° F. Serves 8.

Danish Cockscombs

1 pkg. refrigerator crescent rolls
½ C apricot preserves
Nutmeg to taste
1 egg white
1/3 C sugar
1/3 C chopped almonds

Unroll rectangles of crescent dough. Do not divide in triangles; press perforations to seal. Cut each rectangle in half. Place a spoonful of preserves in center of each square. Sprinkle with nutmeg. Fold in half and pinch edges to seal. Place seam side down on ungreased cookie sheet. With scissors snip half way through each roll along long side. Fan out cut edge slightly. Brush rolls with egg white slightly beaten with 1 T water. Sprinkle with mixture of sugar and nuts. Bake 10 minutes at 375° F. Makes 8.

Edelweis Rolls

Follow instructions for Danish Cockscombs above, but substitute almond filling for apricot preserves.

Blueberry Nut Loaf

1 pkg. (13½ oz.) blueberry muffin mix
2/3 C milk
1 egg
1 C chopped walnuts
¼ C sugar
1/8 t cinnamon

Remove blueberries; rinse and drain on paper towels. Blend milk and egg together and stir into muffin mix. Quickly fold in nuts and blueberries (batter should be lumpy). Pour into a greased 5 x 9-inch loaf pan. Mix sugar and cinnamon and sprinkle over top. Bake 50 minutes at 375° F. Cool before slicing. Serves 8.

Caramel Apple Buns

2 T butter, melted
¼ C brown sugar
½ can (20 oz.) apple slices, drained
2 T raisins
1 pkg. refrigerator raisin cinnamon rolls
Cinnamon to taste

Combine brown sugar and butter; spoon into 8 greased muffin tins. Arrange apple slices and raisins on brown sugar mixture. Top with a cinnamon roll. Bake 15 to 20 minutes at 375° F. Buns will be medium dark brown. Let stand 2 minutes before carefully inverting pan and removing buns. Sprinkle a dash of cinnamon into icing container, stir to mix. Spoon icing over hot buns. Makes 8 buns.

Orange Sticks

8 slices white bread
1/3 C orange juice concentrate, undiluted
1 C sugar
Grated orange peel to taste

Remove crusts from bread and spread with mixture of orange concentrate and sugar. Sprinkle with grated orange peel. Cut each slice in 3 strips, place on cookie sheet and bake 10 minutes at 350° F. Makes 24 sticks.

Blueberry Coffee Cake

1 pkg. hot roll mix, prepared as directed
1 can (20 oz.) blueberry pie filling
1 T lemon juice

After hot roll dough has raised once, roll out on floured surface to fit a 12 x 17-inch jelly roll pan. Add lemon juice to pie filling and spread over dough. Let rise about 20 minutes. Bake 25 to 30 minutes at 375° F. Dribble on a thin confectioners' sugar icing, if desired. Serves 12.

Petit Pains Au Chocolat

1 pkg. hot roll mix or yeast coffee cake mix, prepared as directed
2 T soft butter
12 oz. sweet chocolate (or 1 pkg., 12 oz. chocolate chips)
1 egg, beaten

After first rising, punch down and turn out roll mix on floured surface. Roll out ¼ inch thick and cut in 3-inch rounds. Pat each round of dough into a 4-inch oval, spread with soft butter. Place a ½-oz. square of chocolate in the center of each oval. Pinch together lengthwise edges, enclosing chocolate. Place seam-side down on greased cookie sheet. Brush with beaten egg and let rise until double in bulk. Bake 15 minutes at 350° F. Serve warm. If served later, sprinkle with a few drops of water; reheat in foil. Makes 20 to 22 rolls.

Raised Doughnuts

1 pkg. hot roll mix or yeast coffee cake mix
1 T grated lemon rind
½ t cinnamon
½ t nutmeg

Prepare mix as directed, but add remaining ingredients to dry mixture. Let rise as directed. Punch down dough and turn onto floured surface. Roll or pat dough ½ inch thick. Cut with floured doughnut cutter. Place on floured surface to rise. When double in size, fry in hot fat—370° F. Brown one side, then the other. Drain on paper towels. Ice with confectioners' icing or sprinkle with sugar. Makes 24.

Christmas Fruit Loaf

1 pkg. hot roll mix
½ C preserved, diced, mixed fruit
½ C chopped walnuts
1 t grated lemon rind

Prepare hot roll mix as directed, but blend in fruit, nuts and lemon rind with the flour mixture. Let rise until double in bulk. Turn out on floured surface and knead 1 minute. Shape in loaf and transfer to greased 9 x 5-inch loaf pan. Let rise again. Bake 45 minutes at 375° F. Spread confectioners' sugar icing over top while warm. Serves 8.

Cinnamon Nut Loaf

1 loaf frozen bread dough, thawed
2 T butter, melted
¼ C sugar
½ t cinnamon
½ C chopped nuts or raisins
Melted butter
1 T sugar

Allow thawed dough to rise. Punch down and roll the dough to 10 x 12 inches on a floured surface. Spread dough with melted butter, sprinkle with mixture of cinnamon, sugar and nuts. Roll up dough from the shortest side and fold ends under. Place in a greased 5 x 9-inch loaf pan, seam side down. Let rise until double in size. Brush top with about 1 T melted butter and sprinkle with 1 T sugar. Bake as directed on bread package. Serves 8.

Crullers

1 pkg. refrigerator turnover pastries
Cooking oil, 1-inch deep in electric fry pan

Unroll dough. Cut each square in 1-inch strips. Heat oil to 375° F. Twist strips of dough once or twice and fry a few at a time in hot fat. Fry until brown on one side (about one minute), turn and brown the other side. Drain on paper towels. Sprinkle with powdered sugar or spread the enclosed icing over the pastries. Refrigerate fruit filling and use another day. Makes 32 crullers.

Snowflake Doughnuts

1 pkg. refrigerator fan-tan type yeast rolls

Divide dough into 18 sections. Punch hole in center of
each section. Fry in hot fat, 1½ inches deep, 360° F. Do
not crowd. Fry until brown on one side; turn and brown
the other side. Drain on paper towels. Sprinkle with cinnamon and sugar mixture when cool. Use this method also
with refrigerator buttermilk biscuits. Makes 18.

* * * * *

PUDDINGS

Danish Rum Pudding

1 pkg. golden egg custard
1¾ C milk
3 T rum
1 t lemon juice
1 pkg. (5¼ oz.) fluffy white frosting mix
1 pkg. (10 oz.) frozen raspberries, thawed

Combine custard mix and milk. Cook as directed on mix
package. Remove from heat, stir in rum and lemon juice.
Cool 10 minutes. Prepare frosting mix as directed. Fold
slightly thickened custard mix into frosting mix. Pour into
greased mold or sherbet glasses. Chill. To serve, top with
raspberries. Serves 6 to 8.

Old Fashioned Prune Whip

1 pkg. vanilla dessert mix, prepared as directed
1 can (12 oz.) prune filling
½ C miniature marshallows (optional)

Beat prune filling into prepared dessert mix. Fold in marshmallows, if desired. Serves 6.

Chocolate Soufflé

1 pkg. chocolate pudding and pie filling
Dash salt
3 eggs, separated
1¼ C milk
1 t vanilla

Blend pudding mix, salt, beaten egg yolks and milk. Cook and stir over medium heat until mixture comes to a full boil. Remove from heat and stir until smooth. Cool 5 minutes, and add vanilla. Beat egg whites to soft peaks. Fold into pudding. Pour into a 1-quart greased baking dish. Set baking dish in a pan of hot water. Bake 1 hour at 350° F. Serve hot or cold. Serves 4.

Wine Custard (Weinschaum)

1 pkg. golden egg custard mix
1½ C milk
½ C sherry

Cook custard mix with milk according to directions on package. Remove from heat and gradually stir in sherry. Pour into individual serving dishes and chill. Serves 3 or 4.

Glorified Rice

1 can (13½ oz.) pineapple tidbits, plus juice
1 C instant rice
¾ t salt
6 maraschino cherries, diced
2 envelopes whipped topping mix, prepared as directed
1 C miniature marshmallows

Add enough water to pineapple juice to make 1¼ cups. Bring liquid to boil, stir in rice and salt. Cover, remove from heat and let stand 5 minutes. Add cherries and pineapple; chill thoroughly. Fold prepared topping mix and marshmallows into rice mixture. Serves 8 to 10.

Jean's Pot De Creme

1 pkg. (6 oz.) chocolate chips
2 T sugar
Pinch salt
1 egg
1 t vanilla or rum flavoring
¾ C milk

Place all ingredients except milk in blender. Heat milk just to boiling and pour into blender. Blend 1 minute. Pour immediately into 6 serving dishes or chocolate pots. Chill, if desired, and serve with a dab of whipped cream. Serves 6.

Rice Pudding

1 pkg. real egg custard
2 C milk
¼ C instant rice
¼ C white raisins
Nutmeg to taste

Combine custard mix and milk in a 1-quart baking dish. Stir to dissolve. Add rice and raisins; sprinkle with nutmeg. Bake as directed on package. Serve hot or cold. Serves 6.

Strawberry Bavarian

2 pkgs. strawberry whipped dessert mix
1 C cold milk
½ C water
1 C sour cream
1 pkg. (12 oz.) frozen strawberries

Add cold milk to dessert mix and beat 1 minute. Add water and sour cream, beat 1 minute. Chill in a 1½-quart mold several hours. Unmold on a shallow serving dish and spoon thawed strawberries over mold. Or, mold in a 6-cup ring and fill center with 1 pint fresh strawberries, sliced. Serves 8.

Almond Custard with Apples

1 can (14 oz.) apple slices
1 pkg. golden egg custard mix, prepared as directed
½ t almond extract
¼ C slivered, toasted almonds

Drain apple slices and arrange in attractive serving bowl.
Add almond extract to prepared custard mix. Pour over
apples. Top with a sprinkling of toasted almonds. Serves 6.

Golden Apple Pudding

1 can (20 oz.) apple pie filling
1 pkg. vanilla tapioca pudding mix
1 C apricot nectar
1 T lemon juice

Blend all ingredients, and bring to a boil. Simmer over low
heat 10 minutes, stirring often. Chill and serve. Serves 4.

Orange Delight

1 pkg. (3 oz.) orange gelatin
1 bottle (16 oz.) orange pop
1 envelope whipped topping mix, prepared as directed

Dissolve gelatin in 1 C hot pop. Add remaining cold pop.
Chill until gelatin begins to thicken. Fold into prepared
topping. Chill. Garnish with whipped cream and candied
orange peel. Serves 4.

Pineapple Parfait

1 pkg. pineapple instant pudding, prepared as directed
1 can (20 oz.) pineapple pie filling

Alternate spoonfuls of pudding and pie filling in tall
glasses. Serve cold. Serves 4 to 6.

Italian Chocolate Cheese Dessert

1 lb. ricotta cheese
2 T superfine sugar
¼ C light rum
¼ C chocolate shot (sprinkles)

Beat cheese until soft. Stir in remaining ingredients, reserving 1 t shot for garnish. Chill thoroughly. Serves 4.

For additional pudding recipes, see:
Corn Pudding, p. 86
Hot Blueberry Crumble, p. 142

*   *   *   *   *

FROZEN DESSERTS

For easier serving and better eating allow frozen desserts to stand 15 minutes at room temperature before serving.

Tortoni

1 quart vanilla ice cream, slightly softened
6 coconut macaroons, crushed
1½ T sherry
2 T macaroon crumbs or slivered almonds

Whip ice cream with electric mixer. Add macaroons and sherry. Spoon mixture into molds or paper muffin cups. Sprinkle with 2 T of crumbs or almonds and freeze. Serves 10 to 12.

Blueberry Ice Cream

1 quart vanilla ice cream
1 can (21 oz.) blueberry pie filling

Soften ice cream by stirring. (Do not melt.) Blend in filling and refreeze. Serves 8 to 10.

Frozen Lime Pudding

1 can (1 lb.) fruit cocktail, including liquid
1 pkg. lime or lemon pudding and pie filling
¾ C sugar
1 egg
1 envelope whipped topping mix, prepared as directed
½ C chopped pecans

Drain fruit, reserving liquid. Add enough water to liquid to make 2¼ cups. Combine pudding, sugar and ¼ cup liquid in a saucepan. Add egg and blend well. Stir in remaining liquid. Cook, stirring constantly, over medium heat until mixture comes to a boil. Chill 1 hour. Blend prepared topping into pudding mixture. Add fruit and nuts. Pour into an 8 x 4-inch loaf pan and freeze. Place in refrigerator 30 minutes before serving. Serves 6.

Ice Cream Sandwiches

8 frozen waffles
1 pint ice cream
1 can ready-to-eat frosting

Cut ice cream in 4 slices to fit waffles. Spread frozen waffles with frosting. Place an ice cream slice between 2 waffles, frosting side to the inside. Or, make open face sandwiches (use 1 waffle for each slice of ice cream) and serve with a sweet topping; see p. 160. Serve immediately or refreeze. Serves 4.

Rum Raisin Ice Cream

1 C white raisins
½ C light rum
1 quart rich vanilla ice cream

Combine raisins and rum in a covered container overnight or longer. Pour off any excess liquid from raisins and stir into slightly softened ice cream. Return to freezer to harden. Serves 8.

Rainbow Meringues

1 pkg. fluffy white frosting mix
¼ C sugar
1 pint lime sherbet
1 pkg. (10 to 16 oz.) frozen sliced strawberries, thawed

Prepare frosting mix as directed, but decrease water to 1/3 cup. When stiff gradually beat in sugar. On a greased, floured cookie sheet shape 4 meringues, making an indentation in the center of each. Bake 1 hour at 225° F. Turn off heat and let meringues stand in oven 1 hour longer. When ready to serve, place a scoop of sherbet in center of each meringue and spoon thawed strawberries on top. Serves 4. (If desired, 8 medium-sized, meringues can be made from this recipe.)

Frozen Fudge

1½ C cold milk
½ C cream (or evaporated milk)
1 pkg. chocolate fudge instant pudding
1 T sugar
¼ C chopped pecans

Combine milk, cream, pudding mix, and sugar. Proceed as directed on pudding package. Fold in nuts and pour into ice tray. Freeze until firm around edges, about 2 hours. Transfer mixture to bowl and beat until smooth but not melted. Freeze 2 to 4 hours. Serves 4.

Cooley's Special
(Hot Fudge Sundae Cake)

1 pkg. chocolate cake mix, (1 layer size) prepared as directed
Vanilla ice cream
1 pkg. chocolate fudge sauce mix, prepared as directed, or see Fudge Sauce p. 161
½ C chopped pecans

Bake cake as directed in an 8-inch pan. Cut in squares squares when cool. Top with scoop of ice cream. Spoon lukewarm fudge sauce over all; sprinkle with pecans and serve. Serves 6.

Frozen Lemons

2 lemons
1 pint lemon sherbet
½ C candied lemon peel, finely diced, or preserved mixed
    fruit

Cut lemons in half and hollow out both sides. Mix softened sherbet and candied lemon peel; spoon into shells. Place lemon "halves" together and freeze at least 2 hours. Serve on glossy green leaves. Serves 6.

Frozen Oranges

Follow directions for frozen lemons, substituting oranges, orange sherbet and candied orange peel.

Frozen Coffee Charlotte

1 C cold milk
¼ C instant coffee powder
2 T coffee liqueur or 1 t vanilla
2 T confectioners' sugar
2 envelopes whipped topping mix
4 ladyfingers, split and cut in half

Combine all ingredients except ladyfingers and beat as directed on topping package. Line sides of 1-quart mold with ladyfinger pieces. Pour topping mixture into mold and freeze until firm. Serves 6.

Cherries Jubilee

1 can (21 oz.) cherry pie filling, or 2 pkgs. (10 oz. each)
  frozen cherries, plus juice
Red food coloring
¼ C brandy
1 quart rich vanilla ice cream

Heat cherry filling and a drop or two of red food coloring
in a chafing dish. When ready to serve pour brandy over
cherries and ignite. When flames die down spoon over individual servings of vanilla ice cream. Serves 6.

Lime Sherbet

2 egg whites
¼ C sugar
1 can (6 oz.) frozen limeade concentrate
Green food coloring (optional)

Beat egg whites to a stiff peak and gradually beat in sugar.
Fold in limeade and a drop of green food coloring, if desired. Pour into ice tray and freeze. Serves 2 or 3.

For additional frozen desserts, see:
Frozen Fruit Salad p. 100
Grasshopper Pie p. 141
Rocky Road Pie p. 141

* * * * *

TOPPINGS

Custard Sauce

1 pkg. golden egg custard mix

Follow package directions, but increase milk to 2½ cups.
Add a dash of nutmeg if desired. Makes 2½ cups.

Fudge Sauce #1 (hot)

1 pkg. (6 oz.) chocolate chips
½ C heavy cream or evaporated milk
½ t vanilla

Melt chocolate chips in cream over low heat, stirring continuously. Add vanilla. Makes about 1½ cups.

Fudge Sauce #2 (hot)

1 C instant cocoa mix
1/3 C boiling water
1 T butter

Blend ingredients; serve hot. Makes ½ cup.

Fudge Sauce #3 (cold)

1 pkg. instant chocolate pudding
¾ C corn syrup
¾ C evaporated milk

Stir pudding mix into syrup. Gradually add evaporated milk. Let stand 10 minutes or until thickened. Makes 1½ cups.

Fudge Sauce #4 (hot or cold)

1 pkg. chocolate pudding and pie filling mix
½ C sugar
1 C water
2 T butter

Blend first 3 ingredients and cook over low heat, stirring until sugar is dissolved. Cook until mixture comes to a full boil and thickens. Remove from heat, stir in butter. Serve hot or cold. Makes 1½ cups.

Caramel Sauce

Use Fudge Sauce recipe #3 or #4, but substitute butterscotch pudding for chocolate pudding. Makes 1½ cups.

Karen's Brandy Cream Topping

1 envelope whipped topping mix
¼ C cognac
½ C cold milk

Blend ingredients in deep, narrow-bottomed bowl. Whip with electric beater as directed on package. Makes 2 cups.

Sour Cream Topping

1 C sour cream
¼ C confectioners' sugar

Blend ingredients. Serve over cheesecake or as a garnish. Makes 1 cup.

Chocolate Almond Sauce

1 can (12 oz.) almond filling
¾ C chocolate syrup

Combine and serve. Makes 2¼ cups.

Cider Sauce

1 pkg. vanilla or lemon pudding and pie filling mix
3 C apple juice or cider

Dissolve pudding mix in ¼ C cider. Combine with remaining cider and cook over medium heat until mixture bubbles and thickens. Serve warm over gingerbread, apple pie, turnovers, etc. Makes 3 cups.

Lemon Sauce

1 pkg. lemon pudding and pie filling mix
½ C sugar
1 egg, slightly beaten
3 C water
2 T butter

Blend pudding mix, sugar, egg, and ¼ cup of water. Add remaining water, and cook over medium heat until mixture boils. Remove from heat, and add butter. Serve warm or cold over cake. Makes 3½ cups.

Pineapple Sauce

1 can (8½ oz.) crushed pineapple, plus juice
½ C pancake syrup
Dash salt

Combine ingredients and bring to a boil, stirring occasionally. Serve warm over ice cream, pancakes, etc. Makes 1½ cups.

Cinnamon Sauce

1 can (21 oz.) peach pie filling
1 T red cinnamon candies

Combine ingredients and heat until candies dissolve. Makes 2½ cups.

Apricot Sauce

1 can (12 oz.) apricot filling
½ to 1 C marshmallow creme

Combine and serve. Makes 2 cups.

Basic Sweet Sauce

Boil leftover syrups from any canned fruits 10 minutes. Flavor with vanilla, almond or rum extract to taste.

Chapter 10

Candy

How nice that work-proof candy recipes are mistake-proof too. Making homemade candy these days is almost as much fun as eating it.

Unbeatable Fudge

3 C sugar
½ C butter or margarine
1 can (6 oz.) evaporated milk
1 jar (7 oz.) marshmallow creme
1 large pkg. (12 oz.) chocolate chips
¼ lb. (1 cup) pecans
1 t vanilla

Combine sugar, butter, milk and marshmallow creme in a 3-quart saucepan. Stirring constantly, bring to a rolling boil and cook over medium heat for 5 minutes. Remove from heat and stir in chocolate chips, nuts and vanilla until well blended. Pour into a greased 8 x 12-inch pan. Cool and cut into squares. Makes 3 lbs.

Penuche

2 C sugar
1 C milk
1 jar (7 oz.) marshmallow creme
1 jar (12 oz.) chunk-style peanut butter
1 t vanilla

Combine sugar and milk. Bring to a boil and cook 5 minutes over medium heat to soft ball stage. (238° F.). Remove from heat, add marshmallow creme, peanut butter and vanilla. Beat until well blended. Pour into greased 9-inch square pan. Cool and cut in squares. Makes 2 lbs.

Chocolate Popcorn Balls

1 jar (7 oz.) marshmallow creme
½ C chocolate drink mix
8 C popped corn

Combine marshmallow creme and chocolate in a saucepan, stirring constantly; bring just to a boil. Place popcorn in a large greased bowl. Pour chocolate mixture over popcorn and stir until thoroughly blended. Using greased hands, shape in 3-inch balls. Place on waxed paper and allow to set. Makes 8 to 10 popcorn balls.

Fudge Nuts

1¾ C pecan halves
3 T sugar
¼ t salt
3 T chocolate drink mix

Cover pecans with hot water; drain. Sprinkle with sugar and salt, mixing well. Sprinkle with chocolate and stir until nuts are well coated. Spread in a shallow pan. Heat in a 350° F. oven 15 minutes or until brown. Makes ½ lb.

Pecan Roll

1 jar (7 oz.) marshmallow creme
1 t vanilla
¼ t almond extract
1 lb. confectioners' sugar
1 lb. light caramels (or light and dark combination)
2 lbs. chopped pecans

Add extracts to marshmallow creme and gradually knead in sugar. Shape fondant into 4 to 6 1-inch diameter cylinders, wrap, and freeze solid. Melt caramels in double boiler. Dip frozen fondant cylinders in hot melted caramel. Immediately roll in chopped nuts. Cool. Wrap and tie with bright ribbons and give as Xmas gifts. Makes 4½ lbs.

Sherry Walnuts

1½ C sugar
½ C sherry
½ t cinnamon
3 C walnuts

Boil sugar and sherry to a soft ball stage (238° F.). Remove from heat, add cinnamon and walnuts. Stir until cloudy. Turn out on a greased cookie sheets. Separate and allow to cool. Makes 1½ lbs.

Rocky Road

18 oz. chocolate chips
2 C miniature marshmallows
1¼ C chopped nuts

Melt chocolate in a double boiler. Spread one third of the melted chocolate in a foil-lined 8-inch pan. Cover with mixture of marshmallows and nuts. Pour remaining chocolate over all, stirring slightly to completely coat nuts and marshmallows. Let stand until firm, before cutting in squares. Makes 1 2/3 lbs. of candy.

Satin Fudge

1 lb. sifted confectioners' sugar
1 pkg. (8 oz.) cream cheese, softened
½ C chopped nuts
4 envelopes (1 oz. each) pre-melted unsweetened chocolate
1 t vanilla
Dash salt

Gradually add sugar to softened cream cheese. Blend well. Stir in remaining ingredients. Press in a greased 8-inch square pan. Chill and cut in squares. Makes about 2 lbs.

Caramel Corn Balls

1 pkg. (14 oz.) caramels
¼ C water
4 quarts popped corn, salted

Melt caramels with water in a double boiler. Stir to mix and pour over popcorn. Moisten hands with cold water and shape into balls. Allow to set before eating. Makes 16 to 20 caramel corn balls.

Butterscotch Crunch

1 C butterscotch bits
½ C peanut butter
1 can (3 oz.) chow mein noodles
1 C miniature marshmallows (or peanuts)

Melt butterscotch bits and peanut butter in a double boiler. Stir in noodles and marshmallows. Drop by the spoonful on waxed paper. Chill to set. Makes about 1 lb.

Chocolate Tingalings

1 large pkg. (12 oz.) chocolate chips
1 C salted peanuts
1 can (3 oz.) chow mein noodles

Melt chocolate in a double boiler. Pour over a mixture of nuts and noodles. Toss gently to coat and drop from a teaspoon onto waxed paper. Chill to harden. Makes 2¼ lbs.

Chapter 11

Appetizers and Party Jare

Hors d'Oeuvres
Cold Dips
Hot Dips
Spreads

Note to the party-giver: this chapter is designed to take the nerves out of entertaining, preserve your energy, and keep you out of the kitchen. Attend your own parties—they're more fun that way!

Hostess tips:

1. Whenever possible cook your party food ahead of time; chill in the refrigerator or freeze. Simply reheat to serve the day of the party.
2. Keep dinner party menus simple by cutting down on courses. Often, a large, crunchy tossed salad can be substituted for the hot vegetable dishes your guests will never miss.
3. *Never* wear yourself out cleaning the house on party day. Better the hostess sparkles than the house.

* * * * *

HORS D'OEUVRES

Barbecued Cocktail Franks

1 pkg. (8 oz.) cocktail sausages
1 C barbecue sauce

Simmer sausages in barbecue sauce until glazed (about 30 minutes). Serve hot with toothpicks. Makes 24.

Lynn's Bacon Crisps

If I had come across the recipe for Bacon Crisps before I had seen and tasted them I think I might have passed it up, never guessing the degree of change that would occur during the baking process. The cracker literally absorbs the bacon, taking on all of its flavor and just the right amount of fat to bake to a rich golden brown. The prosaic saltine is completely transformed.

½ lb. bacon (12 strips, cut in half)
24 saltine crackers (standard squares)

Wrap each cracker with a half strip of bacon. Place on a cookie rack over a shallow drip pan. Bake 12 to 15 minutes, turning once, at 400° F. Serve hot. Makes 24.

Hot Olive Cheese Balls

1 stick pie crust mix (pie crust mix for 1 shell)
1 C grated sharp Cheddar cheese (¼ lb.)
½ t paprika
24 stuffed olives

Mix together pie crust mix, cheese and paprika. Wrap each olive with a teaspoon of dough. Freeze cheese balls. Bake frozen at 400° F. for 10 to 15 minutes on an ungreased cookie sheet. Serve hot with toothpicks. Makes 24.

Cocktail Peppers

The bite is in the anchovy paste—the peppers are quite mild.

1 bottle (12 oz.) salad peppers (peperoncini)
1 tube (2 oz.) anchovy paste

Make a lengthwise slit in each pepper and allow them to drain. Fill peppers by squeezing a strip of anchovy paste through the slit. Serve cold. Makes about 2 dozen.

Pâté Wellington

1 lb. liver sausage
2 T Worcestershire sauce
½ C frozen chopped chives, or finely chopped green onion
1 pkg. refrigerator crescent rolls
1 egg, beaten slightly

Mash liver sausage and stir in Worcestershire sauce and chives. Unwrap crescent rolls but do not divide in triangles. Place rectangles side by side to form 2 squares, each 7 inches square. Pinch edges and press perforations to seal. Place half of liver sausage mixture on each square and shape in 2-inch cylinders. Enclose cylinders in pastry, pinching seam to seal. Fold ends neatly. Place loaves on an ungreased baking sheet, seam side down. Brush tops with beaten egg and prick crust to allow steam to escape. Bake 20 minutes at 375° F. or until crust is nicely brown. To serve, place on a wooden tray and provide a small sharp knife to cut slices. Pâté Wellington may be served hot, warm or at room temperature. Each loaf serves 8.

Cheese Cocktail Cookies

1 jar (5 oz.) sharp Old English cheese (processed Cheddar)
1 stick pie crust mix (about 1 C)

Combine cheese and pie crust mix. Shape in marble size balls, flatten with a fork on an ungreased cookie sheet. Chill 30 minutes. Bake 8 minutes at 450° F. Makes 35. Also serve these with a fruit salad at a party luncheon.

Clam Snacks

1 pkg. (7 oz.) frozen French fried clams
½ C seafood Cocktail Sauce, p. 49 (or bottled product)

Heat clams according to package instructions. Heat the cocktail sauce and use as a hot dunk for the clams. Makes 36 bit-size snacks.

Chicken Livers and Bacon (Rumaki)

An old favorite. So fast, so good, so easy it had to be included.

½ lb. chicken livers
½ lb. bacon

Cut chicken livers in 1-inch squares. Cut bacon strips in half. Wrap livers in bacon, securing with a toothpick. Place in a shallow pan. Bake 20 minutes at 350° F. or until bacon is crisp. Drain fat. Serve hot. Makes 24 bite-size hors d'oeuvres. Variations: A.) Pineapple chunks or water chestnuts may be wrapped with the chicken livers and bacon. B.) Scallops or whole mushrooms may be substituted for the chicken livers.

Drumstick Hors d'Oeuvres

16 chicken wings
¼ C melted butter
Salad Supreme seasoning

Have the butcher remove the first joint from each wing, leaving second joint and wing tip intact. Refrigerate first joints and use another time. Holding the wing tip dip the meaty joint in melted butter, sprinkle with Salad Supreme, and arrange on a baking sheet. Bake in a 350° F. oven for 45 minutes. Serve hot. Makes 16.

Hot Sweet Sauce

1 jar (10 oz.) currant jelly
1 jar (6 oz.) prepared mustard

Melt jelly over low heat and stir in mustard until well blended. Serve hot or cold as a dunking sauce with shrimp, meatballs, sausage, egg rolls, fried clams, etc. Makes 2 cups.

Pizza Canapes

1 pkg. refrigerator butterflake rolls (fan-tan type yeast rolls)
1 envelope spaghetti sauce mix
1 can (1 lb.) tomatoes
1 clove garlic, crushed
½ C Parmesan cheese, grated
2 T minced anchovy fillets

Divide each of 18 pieces of dough into 2 layers. Place 36 thin biscuits on a greased cookie sheet. Bake 7 minutes at 375° F. Do not remove from cookie sheet. Meanwhile, combine sauce mix, tomatoes and garlic in a saucepan and simmer 20 minutes. Place a tablespoon of spaghetti sauce on each biscuit, sprinkle with Parmesan cheese and top with a pinch of minced anchovy. Broil until bubbling. Serve hot. Makes 36 canapes. (Flaky Refrigerator biscuits may be substituted and separated in the same way. One package will make 24 thin biscuits. Bake 8 minutes at 400° F.)

Pastry Surprises

1 pkg. refrigerator turnover pastries
Small marinated shrimp, salted pecans, stuffed olives, bite-
    sized sausage slices, pitted ripe olives, smoked oysters,
    etc.

Set aside fruit filling and icing for another use. Unroll turnover dough and cut each square into four squares or triangles. Wrap one of the suggested fillings in each piece of dough. Pinch edges to seal. Bake 7 minutes at 400° F. Serve hot with Hot Sweet Sauce below. Makes 32 canapes.

Marinated Mushrooms

Whole mushrooms in a jar
Ceasar salad dressing

Open jar and drain mushrooms. Replace liquid with salad

dressing. Replace cap and refrigerate mushrooms at least 3 hours before serving.

Hot Mushroom Canapes

1 pkg. refrigerator turnover pastries (use dough only)
1 lb. mushrooms, chopped
¼ C butter
1 t salt
½ C bread crumbs (about)

Use turnover pastry dough only; put aside fruit filling and icing for other uses. Sauté chopped mushrooms in butter until tender, 5 to 10 minutes. Sprinkle with salt. Stir in bread crumbs until butter and juices are absorbed. Unroll pastry squares. Spoon mushroom mixture in a strip in the center of each square. Bring parallel edges of pastry together, overlapping slightly. Cut each roll in 4 slices. Place slices on an ungreased cookie sheet and flatten slightly. Bake at 400° F. for 7 minutes or until nicely brown. Makes 32 flaky morsels.

Cocktail Meatballs

1½ lbs. ground beef
3 bread slices, cubed
1 envelope chili mix
1 egg
¾ C milk
1 envelope spaghetti sauce mix, prepared as directed

Blend all ingredients except spaghetti sauce mix well. Shape into 72 one-inch balls. Place on a jelly roll pan (11 x 16 inches) and bake 15 minutes at 450° F. Drain. Transfer meatballs to a chafing dish and pour hot spaghetti sauce over them. Serve hot, and don't forget the toothpicks. Makes 72 meatballs.

Cocktail Roll-Ups

1 pkg. cocktail franks (24)
1 pkg. refrigerator crescent rolls
Prepared mustard

Unroll dough and spread with mustard. Divide along perforations into 8 triangles. Cut each triangle into three triangles. Wrap each sausage in a small triangle, rolling up according to crescent directions. Bake 10 minutes at 375° F. Makes 24 roll-ups.

* * * * *

COLD DIPS

Alexander Dip

1 pint sour cream
1 T mayonnaise
1 can (12 oz.) pineapple cake and pastry filling
Pinch salt

Blend well and serve cold. Makes 3½ cups.

Basic Onion Dip

1 pint sour cream
1 envelope onion soup mix

Stir onion soup mix into the sour cream and chill in the refrigerator at least an hour. Makes 2 cups.

Mystery Dip

1 can (4½ oz.) chopped ripe olives
2/3 C mayonnaise

Combine and serve chilled. Makes about 1½ cups.

$1,000 AWARD
FOR YOUR FAVORITE RECIPE

A recipe you are using right now or one that may have been in the family for generations may be just what we're looking for. We're reviewing recipes for the next edition of Potpourri of Cookery. Recipes submitted and approved may be published in this unique cookbook made up entirely of these great recipes.

We would like to review your recipe and if approved you are eligible to win one of our CASH AWARDS UP TO $1,000. Please send only one recipe entry per family (any kind are eligible from appetizers to desserts).

We're not looking for recipes from professional chefs. A simple recipe may be the next winner—let us be the judge. The review service is free, easy way to find out if your recipe is a winner.

FREE ENTRY COUPON
ON OTHER SIDE

Mail to:
**Treasured Recipes
c/o FLEET & MORGAN
200 Madison Avenue
New York, NY 10016**
YES! Please enter my recipe and notify
me if it is accepted for publication.

PLEASE PRINT CLEARLY

NAME _____

ADDRESS _____

CITY _____

STATE _____ZIP _____

Name of
Recipe _____